FROM
Faith TO
Faith

AS WE LIVE IN THE SPIRIT

To my dear friends
Mike and Kay –

Marie

MARIE HUNTER ATWOOD

Author of *And There Was War in Heaven*

WESTBOW
PRESS®
A DIVISION OF THOMAS NELSON
& ZONDERVAN

Scripture taken from the New King James Version. Copyright © 1979, 1980, 1982 by Thomas Nelson, Inc. Used by permission. All rights reserved.

WestBow Press books may be ordered through booksellers or by contacting:

WestBow Press
A Division of Thomas Nelson & Zondervan
1663 Liberty Drive
Bloomington, IN 47403
www.westbowpress.com
1 (866) 928-1240

ISBN: 978-1-4908-7337-4 (sc)
ISBN: 978-1-4908-7338-1 (hc)
ISBN: 978-1-4908-7336-7 (e)

Library of Congress Control Number: 2015904067

Print information available on the last page.

WestBow Press rev. date: 08/12/2015

I am so grateful to all the Christians in the world
For their faith and their perseverance—
For the love that has been their motivation
As they have obeyed the commandment
"Feed my sheep."

His Image—Our Example
"Let us make man in our image, according to our likeness"
"So God created man in His own image …
Male and female He created them."
—Genesis 1:26

Transformed by His Image
"But we all with unveiled face,
Beholding as in a mirror the glory of the Lord,
Are being transformed into the same image from
Glory to Glory,
Just as by the Spirit, the Lord."
—2 Corinthians 3:18

Contents

Awe

What is awe? "Awe is a sense of transcendence for the purpose of perceiving intimations of the divine."[1] Such is the magnificence allowed us through this perception of what "might be" that man becomes creative in the ability he possesses, but at the same time he begins to draw away from that far away realm and from God, who was his inspiration. He is impressed now with his own ability.

His ability to transcend lessens, but again he looks to his own abilities and marvels at the breadth of his accomplishments. After all, what he is no longer able to comprehend awaits his own "discovery." But an interesting thing happens: as he begins to realize the truth of the promise that "it is appointed for man once to die," he begins to feel his bones grow old with the knowledge that his youth is long flown away to a land no longer known. Others are making the discoveries that once were his, and for some reason, work seems to have lost its luster. He is vague about what had filled him with enthusiasm and the desire to climb his own ladder so that he could peer downward at those beneath him.

Was it too late to turn around? What were discoveries and creations except pain and worry, fear and loneliness, and suddenly he remembered a phrase that used to float in his head: "to sense the ultimate in the common and the simple; to feel in the rush of passing, the stillness of eternity," and he knew at last that "what cannot be comprehended by analysis, one may always become aware of by awe."[2] If only he had waited.

---

[1]   Abraham Joshua Heschel, *I Asked for Wonder, A Spiritual Anthology*, ed. Samuel H. Dresner (New York: The Crossroad Publishing Co., 1983), 3

[2]   Heschel, *I Asked for Wonder, A Spiritual Anthology*, 3.

Why is awe so important? Without it, what is extraordinary appears to us as habit, the dawn a daily routine without 'how' echoing in our minds. Does this correlate with the God whose presence surrounds us in incredible beauty and with the wonder of it all? Unfortunately, many spend inordinate amounts of time claiming ownership of their personal "discoveries," never realizing or admitting it was not a discovery at all but a revelation to be used, as well as a revelation that demanded awesome gratitude to God. Without the gratitude that exudes the awesome nature of God, guess who will take credit for all that He has done? Discovery is often a continuation of man's feeling that he is his own God.

As this attitude grew, so too did the memory man had of an awesome God. Every time God is pushed away as insignificant, man's character undergoes a change, and he begins to lose his need of God. His morals deteriorate, his compassion evaporates, his language shows his "goodness," and his creativity evaporates. Where has his awe gone?

I see this not as a deliberate degeneration of man but as the arrogance of ignorance. How can we see the ineffable when we have ceased to see the trees that provide shade for a yard, for birds, for children, or the incredible beauty of all creation—the mountains that reach heavenward into spaces of intense blue, valleys sprinkled with wild-flowers and animals that do what they were created to do, and in so doing, offer thanks for their creation.

I am put in remembrance of a certain day, clear and sunny, when earth suddenly appeared on our television screens, and there was a moment of awe throughout the world. For some, it probably lingered for more than a moment, but within days, the unexpected visual was a moment forgotten. Surely the world hung there with no help, no straps, without giant hooks yet graceful, colorful, hanging on nothing in the space God had created. As it hung there—decidedly on nothing—it spoke to us of the Father, of God the Almighty who was in His heavens, watching, as we observed the majesty of what He had created for us.

Gloriously it hung. Amazingly, it was calm and serene. Must I remind you that that view was not just the world in which we live? No, it included all people and all animals, but I realized belatedly, as it hung there it holds even more than what's yours, mine, and 'his'. It contains everything that has been made and everything that has been created since—all that God or man has made. That magnificent sphere contains it all. Within it, is the structure created by Him, plus the structure of man's "improvements." In fact, it contains both the living and the dead. As you contemplate the size, the weight and the breadth of the sphere we call home, you can better understand that our God knows everything as He possesses all power, and never dies. He lives throughout the ages, as if it is all happening at once.

Let it fill your mind with awe, and let that same awe keep you close beside Him, not only in order to benefit from His blessings but to grow in the ability to praise Him as He deserves to be praised. This awesome matter that He created for us has no need for the traditionally marked "Made in USA" signage in order to claim its authenticity. It hangs quietly, proclaiming by the dignity of being its lack of need for such traditionally marked claims on workmanship, for it was obvious to all that no one but God could have made this beauty.

Any architect in the world would have loved to have been the all-important person who could claim responsibility for what hung there in space, yet very few even thought to praise God, the Creator.

Against a vast background of the darkest black, we were allowed to witness what He had done, yet in such a short time it was as if nothing had been seen. To mankind it was as if nothing had occurred. We experienced it, and then we forgot it. Did any of us think of God in that moment? Did we praise Him at least for a moment? Make no mistake, it was a moment of omnipotence, did you recognize it? How many of us around the world exclaimed, as we fell to our knees "Oh Lord, how magnificent is your name in all the earth"? Did we even ponder its significance? I don't know your answers to these questions, but I do know that they are important ones. Ask yourself the questions and think about your answers, because He wants to know from *you* how you feel, even though He is already quite knowledgeable regarding the condition of your heart.

The modern mind probably doesn't agree that God still works behind the scenes as He did in the book of Daniel or the book of Esther or for that matter throughout the Bible. We like to believe (usually at times when everything is going well) that we are completely in control of our lives; but in reality, we are not. He gives us many examples in which He informs us over and over again that He will not wait forever for us to acknowledge Him.

What is the significance to God of the awe we owe Him? To me, it is very simple: He loves us and wants the entire world to see the sphere in which we live and breathe and have our being. It is a creation of such magnificence, such awe. Does He not deserve credit for the incredible manner in which it hangs unattached—the lack of both reason and knowledge can beset us if we contemplate this unequal balance of power but instead we become demanding for all the answers, yet the whys are still beyond our understanding. It is then that we can be overcome with a feeling of inadequacy, and instead of praising Him, there are those who resent it. Yet the manner in which it hangs on nothing is quite beyond our knowledge and reason, and it extends the time in which we can come to know Him. He wants us to *know* without doubt that this world was created *by* Him and that it is His creation *for us*. He wants us to recognize the extent to which He "does" for us, and *if* we have the correct attitude about that, we will *want* to praise Him. Why do we choose *not* to? I think it is because it requires a submissive attitude and an humble spirit, so we scoff at awe and allow resentment to become a part of us.

Awe is so important, because only awe can keep us aware of the differences between God and man. It informs us, at least on a subconscious level, of who He is and what he does; it keeps us close to Him, allowing us to have a relationship and the ability to build on that relationship. Without awe, we begin to lose moral values; we lose respect for self and others, and soon the heart begins to search for something greater to worship, because without Him, we are not whole. Read in the Old Testament about the gods (idols) that the Israelites worshiped, even to the extent of sacrificing their own children in order to pacify a god that didn't exist, except in their evil minds and in their blood lust.

In spite of man's progress in the challenge of subduing the world, the prospect of that will never be complete, because God reveals small pieces of His knowledge to man as He sees man is ready. I suspect that there is so much more yet to be discovered that it means that man may continue to learn as long as God sees fit. In spite of the number of scientists who are working on various projects on this earth, I'm not too concerned with the range of what their inventions will mean to the world. The information that we, as Christians, have been trusted to share, however, is vital. This is the reason we must learn the best ways to share it.

We are so ignorant regarding many things about which we long to hear. And yet, as some say, the ineffable is beyond the words of language, so why bother? I recall placing a seashell to my ear as a child and imagining huge waves, followed by thunder, as it crashed onto the shore. Even unknowingly, things like that speak to us of God; we have only to open our eyes to see and to praise Him for what we see. And yet we overlook the things God has already given us. We dwell in the midst of grandeur but fail to see it. Why do we not see? One of the biggest reasons is because it has become ordinary to our eyes. We see, but we have ceased to be amazed. The beauty of a sunrise, the beautiful sky and clouds, and—perhaps the most ordinary of all—the beauty that surrounds us all serve a purpose that points to relationship with God, definitely a beginning step in His plan for reconciliation. Let's set goals in which we promise to open our eyes with our hearts and then offer praises to the One who has given even His Son that we might live.

Anything within the sphere of what was created is worthy of praise; perhaps we just need to think about it to see it. Generally unknown to us, the inanimate also has voice. Do we need to praise God for these? Do we praise "the rocks and the rills"? We are told by scientists that the inanimate is never silent. To me, this means that everything has a voice. For instance, we may not hear the voice of mountains—very few people do—but those who seek to understand the ways of mountains will also learn how to hear and interpret their voice. Those who do hear these "voices" often find it impossible to live among them, for they are never silent, and who can understand? It would seem then that instead of considering some things of unequal value, even worthless, we need to understand that this is God's way of granting dignity, even to the inanimate. If you will consider awe as your tool for understanding, you will be granting a measure of dignity to all things, large or small, and in the process, they too stand for something supreme.[3] What does this mean? It means that we, as Christians, can't afford to lose this reaction of recognizing and expressing awe. It is our reaction to awe that provides motivation, a major purpose for spreading God's Word. *Experiencing* awe is not only a great motivator, but it is also a necessity to the hearer, in order that he may *grasp the nature of spirituality.*

---

[3]   Heschel, *I Asked for Wonder, A Spiritual Anthology,* 3.

We often forget that the more we are aware of the ineffable, the more we will see; and the more we see, the more we will be allowed to see; and the more we are allowed to see, the more we will learn; and the more we learn, the more we will know to enable us to learn more. Please think about this, and perhaps there will be many who will again be able to witness the awe that has been lost to them and consequently be strengthened in their faith.

Introduction

Living in the Spirit is the most *critically* important thing a Christian can do in a lifetime. Such living comes from faith in the Lord our God. It is my belief that most of us are believers in God and His Son in our minds, but the question is, do we let that belief into our hearts, thereby *living* for Him, or do we choose to live by the dictates of the flesh that He also gave us to house the person we become? As we are aware, the body is a temporary facility for the soul and spirit, a house in which we dwell. With an added portion of God's Spirit, this is who we are. God's ultimate plan for us is that we grow to be *more* like Him as we prepare for that new spirit body on the order of His own and in which we will dwell with Him in His eternal home. This change of form is what we compare to the term *metamorphosis* in the animal world or more commonly in the human as transformation. Christians must be transformed from what we are to what we *can* be. It can be hypothesized that *belief* is a tentative reaching out to the Creator, but belief alone isn't enough. We know that for the sake of health and the acquisition of wisdom in physical life, there must be physical growth. So it is in the spiritual world. Growth is a necessity that must travel along with spirituality in order for growth of the spirit. Can you imagine a child growing without proper nourishment? It is a relevant comparison and one that could easily be categorized as the key to spiritual growth. We must therefore strengthen our spirit so that we are then *able* to do His will and in that process, He grants not only the ability to grow spiritually but also the blessings that come with spiritual growth.

Our belief in God and our faith that trusts Him and longs for Him *cannot be an abstract acknowledgment.* If we do not acknowledge Him in an active way, we are like the demons who "believed and trembled" (James 2:19 NASB). Why do they tremble? They tremble because *they know He is God, the only God, who is omnipotent, omnipresent, and omniscient.* To acknowledge and stand in awe of Him requires a measure of humility that recognizes His *unique nature*, as well as the selfishness of our own. It recognizes that while He gifted us with a portion of His nature by breathing in our nostrils the breath of life, we are not yet who He wants us to be. If our belief and our longing for Him are nestled in the heart, it will *compel* us to seek Him in order to learn from Him. We do not accomplish this transformation by ourselves, but as we learn and as we adjust our lives accordingly, God actively changes us from the old self to the new self—the spiritual person He still wants us to be. There is an important factor we *must understand.* Seeking doesn't just happen. It requires motivation that comes from the pressing desire of the heart, and without desire there is no motivation and no growth.

The Role of Knowledge

Not surprisingly, *natural knowledge* will kick in as a result of seeking Him. Who, then, is the teacher? An interesting question: if knowledge is a *given result* for the seeker, it tells us that we are taught by the Spirit. "The manifestation of the Spirit is given to each one for the profit of all" (1 Corinthians 12:7). It is gifted to us because of a desire for knowledge and is to be shared with others who also are seeking. This doesn't mean there won't also be human teachers but it levies a heavy restraint on those who would be teachers to speak only as God speaks. The restraint is on the student as well, who must search the Scriptures to determine the accuracy of what's been said. From this we can understand very plainly that responsibility for accuracy rests on both sides.

As an example of this type of teaching, we read of Philip and the Ethiopian eunuch (Acts 8:30–38). God sent Philip to the eunuch because of the eunuch's *desire* to understand what he was reading. Philip was God's messenger and was able to teach the eunuch of Jesus. The eunuch was baptized and went on his way, rejoicing for what he had learned. The Spirit caught Philip away to continue telling the good news of Jesus. This is the same role God gives us in today's world. We are His messengers, just as Philip was. Please notice, however, that Philip was willing to go. This same verse gives us the reason that spreading the gospel news has been placed in human hands. It is our task as children of God to welcome this responsibility.

It was for this reason that Philip was directed to share the good news with the eunuch, even as Saul was directed to the city for the information needed. "We have this treasure in earthen vessels that the excellence of the power may be of God and not of us" (2 Corinthians 4:7). The treasure refers to the gospel; then God uses our knowledge as *divine revelation*. Are you wondering "how so"? If you are studying the Scriptures and are led by the Spirit, it is the Spirit who has taught you. As such, we are His "human vessels" (2 Corinthians 4:7). Our role is to be ready for the opportunities He provides, not to glorify self but to give praise and glory to Him. In bringing those who are *seeking* to Him, God's wisdom is verified again and again, with the result that His kingdom spreads. Do we remember that souls are saved as the *reason* for our learning? I hope that it is continually our purpose and our fulfillment.

A cautionary statement indicates that if the Spirit is *not* your teacher and if you are "learning" from the mouths of man (human teachers), you may or may not have the truth you are seeking. Keep seeking. This is the main reason I hesitate to recommend the use of commentaries until we are well grounded in the truth. Mistakes are a part of our nature as humans and are seldom intentional. However it is similar to the advice we often hear in regard to purchasing products, "let the buyer beware." Caution is never wrong as we seek for what we need, and each of us is responsible for our own salvation.

Faith, Both Substance and Evidence

Learning in this sense is a privilege, because to learn is to do which demonstrates the value of *faith*, which, as we recall, is the ingredient that is capable of moving mountains (1 Corinthians 13:2). Does our Father *literally* mean that faith can remove mountains? Quite probably; it is unfortunate, however, that man has not yet demonstrated a capability for such an awesome faith, so we will instead look at the metaphorical interpretation.

Nature is a wonderful means by which we may draw such meanings. One of the purposes of my book *And There Was War in Heaven* was to point to God's sameness and His continuity. There are many ways in which the laws of nature extend to our spiritual existence. One of the most evident is the manner in which man addresses his relationships with others. We take it for granted that the "substance" of our faith is the criteria on which our belief exists and through which we share with others. We begin with God, but where is the evidence of such a beginning? This may be surprising, but while it begins with our own effort, the evidence of that effort is in the person we are teaching, as manifested by that person's changed life, even as we also show our growth in Him. This is true worship because we are demonstrating both the substance and the evidence of lives lived for Him.

Metamorphosis

In the realm of nature, many processes reveal God's continuity as they reach across human lines that separate us from the lower animals of the world. This is possible because His principles are consistent. In the gospel of John, for instance, we read metaphors that take us into the abstract, such as living waters, life and light, etc. When such instances are understood, they have a profound influence on our spiritual lives. Just to think of such an occurrence can seem almost magical, so I hope this will be inspiring to you as you consider the ramifications that await your decision to grow in faith.

As I have already said, the idea of metamorphosis by itself is magical, having an aura of improbability about it, so I'm hopeful we can carry that feeling into our comparison, which is technically a similitude (from the word simile) because it uses the word "like." We understand that concept, as one thing can often be "like" another thing. A metaphor is more specific than a simile, because while a simile is "like," a metaphor "is," such as in "Jesus is God." Our comparison: "Jesus is *like* a man, but He *is* God." We have an example of each as we focus on the dynamic of this process, so remember the difference between a comparison and something that "is." When metamorphosis is accomplished, and we are presented with our spiritual bodies in eternity, we will be prepared to accept in gracious devotion and will not be required to question, "Is this the real thing?" Am I right?

The Importance of Form

We are talking here of changing our form. Is that at all scary to you? Remember that the house we occupy is temporary, while the new body we shall be given will not waste away. It will be our home with Him in eternity. While the butterfly achieves the result of such a phenomenon through the genetics God has given it, our Lord seems to desire that in the *human body* it will occur by human initiative. Keep in mind that the ultimate transformation for man is the exchange of a physical body for a spiritual body, which will reveal the changed form after it has been declared "perfect."

In the physical world a particular type of insect (a lepidopterist) lays eggs, and from those eggs a caterpillar is hatched, with the shape and form of a worm. Man also begins his journey as an egg, and while the form of an infant is preferable (to us) to beginning as a worm, the simile is that your worth to *God's plan* is still *like* that of a worm. (Remember, God's desire is for fellowship.) The worm, in due time, is changed to the form of a chrysalis, in which it develops in an inanimate manner for a good while, which corresponds somewhat to man's development within the uterus—he is more active physically than the worm but still inanimate in a mental/spiritual capacity. Eventually, the chrysalis opens, and lo and behold, an animal (did you know butterflies are considered animals? I didn't, I'm sorry to say) comes out from the chrysalis with several pairs of feet, four wings with downy scales, an overall covering of fine hairs, and a convoluted tongue in the shape of a spiral. All of these characteristics, plus the incredible beauty of multiple colors, combine in the new form of what *was* a worm. Meanwhile, man emerges from the womb, in which he also has undergone zillions of changes. These changes include bones, muscles, ligaments, skin, hair, and body complete with arms, legs, fingers, toes, and the ability to see, hear, feel, and have voice, as well as all of the other things inside the body that allow him to function as a human. However, from the egg, neither man nor worm is yet as God would have him or it be.

Let's leave this aspect for just a moment in order to observe some other interesting characteristics. When we consider the worm before metamorphosis, we often actually shudder in revulsion. This is possibly because it grovels in the earth or in a body or on plants or other areas, always in a slow, secretive manner that undermines as it insinuates itself into a place for itself. Is this "man" without God? I'm tempted to say so, but it is an incomplete comparison because of man's brain and reasoning ability, whereas the worm is guided by an automatic directive within its worm-like body.

This is the point at which we speak of the growth process, and it is this process that leads to metamorphosis, but what if change doesn't occur? What if we fail to listen to what our body says to us? If the worm doesn't listen, it becomes locked in its chrysalis of darkness until it dies. There is a likeness here in both of these examples that I'm hoping you'll catch, because they don't just apply to the worm. What if our person under discussion never acknowledges God as his Maker, nor accepts the Son as his Savior. In such a situation, that person never exits the darkness in which he lives. Be aware that man can actually be his own greatest enemy because he is egotistical, self-satisfied, arrogant, and envious of those who have more than he thinks they deserve. Are we really like this? I'm afraid so, but God helps us if we will hear His voice and obey.

I am so glad that God brought the butterfly out of the chrysalis as an incredibly beautiful creature, because it could reveal something of our new spiritual form. I don't mean to imply that our bodies will resemble the butterfly *except* in the beauty the butterfly possesses. Have you any idea of the number of different color combinations the butterfly has? I suppose this multiplicity of kinds could also be representative of all the different colors, shapes, and personalities of the people of the world, and if so, there is another possibility. If the similarity is indeed a metaphor rather than a simile, it is *possible* that we will retain the individuality God gave us originally. Since God does not make mistakes, we can look forward to enjoying the fruits of our spirituality in a way that was seldom a part of us as humans.

If we consider the path He has revealed and if we *seek* Him with heart and soul, loving Him and therefore loving all those whom He has created, a metamorphosis or transformation *will* occur. God makes the final changes for us. Until then, it is our responsibility to struggle and learn, to learn and change, to change and be, but all with the help of God. What will we be? We will be alive for Him—excited, full of enthusiasm, and in awe of the Savior, the Father, and the Spirit. It is safe to say that the *desire* for Him is the creative force that allows transformation. That force will help to keep us on the path of seeking and learning as we make progress with living in the obedience of love, which, as Jesus has said, is still the most important commandment (Matthew 22:36–37).

Let's determine, then, that we will not be like the demons, unwilling to manifest the humility that would allow transformation and the acceptance of the responsibility of living for Him. This seems to be a very simple decision. To be with God in a place of no tears and no sorrow, a place of beauty and peace without sin (Revelation 21:4), seems almost beyond the need for a decision, yet throughout the ages, many have rejected the offer.

His Infinite Help

I find it fascinating that we are granted gifts from God that aid the process toward metamorphosis. The breath of life and the indwelling gift of the Holy Spirit both allow us not only to live but also to grow and to become like Him. It should be empowering to us, as followers of Christ, that when we become His follower, He gives us another portion of who He is. We don't have to wonder about that something, as Scripture tells us it is the Holy Spirit who will live within to become our Guide, our Teacher and our Comforter and who assumes many other roles in helping us in the process of removing our habitation from the darkness of the chrysalis to the beauty of life.

It is the Holy Spirit who testifies with our spirit that we belong to Him. "The Spirit Himself bears witness with our spirit that we are children of God" (Romans 8:16). This information is revealed to Him by means of observation of the things we say, do, and think. My observation is that because this demonstrates the changes within *us*, it is likely that His Spirit serves as the embodiment of His nature. This is why we can study His nature as a goal for the changes we need to make in our nature.

One of my favorite texts describes it this way:

"When a person turns to the Lord, the—veil is
taken away.
Now the Lord is the Spirit,
And where the Spirit of the Lord is, there is liberty.
But we all, with unveiled face, beholding –
As in a mirror – the glory of the Lord,
Are being transformed into the same image –
From glory to glory, just as from the Lord,
The Spirit" –
(2 Corinthians 3:16–18).

Keep in mind that the "unveiled face" refers to the "removal of sin by turning to the Lord," and when we do that, God forgives our sin. This takes us to the crucified and resurrected Savior, who paid the price for us by shedding His innocent blood as the payment required and from whom we may understand the reason God now grants forgiveness of sin. No longer does man have to let his sins accumulate for a year, at which time the high priest paid the debt as prescribed by the Lord God by offering the blood of bulls and goats, which allowed those sins to accumulate for another year, year after year, until the sacrifice of Jesus took place.

Having relinquished His human body when He ascended back into heaven, Jesus became the perfect example for us of righteousness and the path we can take—or refuse to take—in *choosing how we shall live.* Such choice grants us the liberty to believe and obey as we live for God or, if we choose to live for Satan, the punishment of sorrow. We are being transformed not just into His likeness but into the essence of His nature. Do you realize that this is what gives us the ability to say, "Thanks, but no thanks" to Satan? I don't need that choice! Isn't that a marvelous verse?

This verse demonstrates the basics of how transformation begins (with change) and where it ends (within man). As we gaze at Him, unburdened by the weight of sin, we are transformed by emulation of His nature. We "gaze" by means of our service to Him, our sacrifice of self, our praise of Him, and our study as we strive to *be* (live) for Him. *That* is the living that opens the chrysalis and exchanges its form to a new spiritual one. That is the goal. The opening of the chrysalis is so powerful that it opens the gates of heaven and a hereafter without pain or sorrow. It offers the marvels of living with the Creator. That has been our task, and then it will be our reward. It accomplishes what we could never have accomplished on our own—eternal life.

Are we resting on the pinnacle of having accepted Him? If we are, we are missing the grandest miracle of all eternity—the metamorphosis of man to spirit and the fulfillment of God's wish for reconciliation and fellowship with man. Without God, man cannot reach for such an ending. On the other hand, God has made it evident that without the cooperation of man, His dream will also fall short of its fullest anticipation.

The Spirit speaking for the Trinity sets before us the goal—the promise of living in the light with our Savior—but He also points to the darkness of the chrysalis in order to urge us forward to accomplish the task before us. It leads me to believe that the gifts God gives man are in some fashion a catalyst for seeking Him. It is from this beginning that man will form an opinion of what has been revealed to him. Will he decide to humble himself and follow God, or will he maintain the supremacy of self-rule and adhere to the dictates of his own flesh, which come from Satan? Remember, that God does not force discipleship. By choosing, man decides if he wants God's gift. This hypothesis, to some extent, explains the presence of evil in our lives. Where does evil come from? I suspect it has always *been —just* as God has always been, and since choice demanded an option, evil was chosen because it is the opposite of good and provides a real difference to good. It doesn't really matter, as the end result is the same: separation from God and ultimately the sacrifice of the Son to enable reconciliation.

A Deeper Motivation

I have come to believe that there is an even deeper motivation for giving man choice. God needed man to ask regarding His identity in order to open the door to man's knowledge of Him. It is obvious that God wanted man to recognize Him as the giver of all that he had. "Who is He?" opened the door by recognizing God's greatness and His singularity, which would enable man to acknowledge his own need. There would be no source from which this recognition could flow unless man could realize God's divine characteristics. Therefore, God made it possible for man to first ask, "Who is He?" And as he realizes that it is God from whom all blessings flow, and that He is the "One who justified the Jews by faith and justified the Gentiles through faith" (Romans 9:30), then he is ready to hear Him. After man *knows* God as Creator, Savior, and Judge, he is more likely to be submissive in obedience, and he will approach God in humility. Without such recognition, he dishonors God, and he fails to obey, and he says, "I don't need anything from God," not realizing how much he receives from Him every day without asking. If you know "who He is", then you are able to recognize what He does for you.

Why do I call this problem a crisis? I do so because each of us progressively travels a path of no return where the Spirit is concerned. It isn't that we have reached a point where it is impossible to have unity with the Father but rather that the physical says to the mental, "We don't need that gift from God. We're doing fine on our own." When this happens, guidance of the spirit virtually shuts down until we discover that we need and want help. I believe this also happens when we ignore the guidance we receive. Many outside influences prompt our curiosity about a God we don't know, but the most effective nudge is from within. Unknown to the world is the fact that the Father has an "agreement" with the human mind that reveals the need to know God. We can quench the need, or we can heed it. God Himself tells us the desire is within us: "for that which is known about God is evident within them; for God made it evident to them" (Romans 1:19).

A Preview of the Model

I thought it would be interesting to preview the model from which we were made. God tells us that we were *created in His image and in His likeness*.[4] "Let us make man in our image, according to our likeness …

---

[4]   Strong's Expanded Exhaustive Concordance, 6754.

so God created them in His own image; in the image of God He created him; male and female he created them" (Genesis 1:26–27). In Genesis 2:7, we are told that man was formed of the dust of the ground, and that God "breathed into his nostrils the breath of life, and man became a living being." In Genesis 1:28, we learn that Adam and Eve were given dominion over birds, fish, and every living thing on the earth. They also were told to fill the earth and subdue it. In addition, we learn that when Adam was 130 years old, he died. Hebrews 9:27 gives the reason: for it is "appointed for men to die but after this the judgment." The situation now is that we don't get to have eternal life unless we choose it.

This 'appointment' did not become a part of life for Adam and Eve until after their sin and their expulsion from the garden. Before that time, physical death was not yet a part of their idyllic life in the garden that God had prepared for them. I wouldn't want you to think (wrongly so) that God acted in an unloving way when He expelled them from the garden. It was an action that *had* to be taken, because they had eaten of the Tree of Life and would have lived forever in a state if darkness, because there was, as yet, no forgiveness of sin. By expelling them, they had a chance to redeem themselves. God always provides a way for this to become reality (Genesis 2:17).

We can learn several things about God here, but first I want to take a peek at the definitions of two words as they relate to creation. By definition, "likeness" has to do with *form, shape,* or *pattern*.[5] The Hebrew for that word was chosen to mean man's "similarity to God."

The word image, as in "made in God's image," is *tselem*, which in the Hebrew means "image, in the sense of one's essential nature,"[6] which is probably both male and female, because both Adam and Eve were created in His image, with each having some of both characteristics. Physically, they are diverse, in order to fulfill the commandment to multiply, yet they are complementary and were designed to be in close harmony. That opinion is just as likely, however, to be an improbability because of the differences in their spiritual/physical patterns. As with so many other things, we will have to wait and see.

---

5   Strong's Expanded Exhaustive Concordance, 1823.
6   Strong's Expanded Exhaustive Concordance, 6754

God commanded Adam to "subdue"[7] the earth (Genesis 1:28), which gives a little different concept than "to have dominion over."[8] Let's examine the difference. Dominion indicates sovereignty, as a king, the "head guy," who has the ruling control but who may not be the ruler. One person might subdue the nation and be the titular head, while someone else might be the right-hand man who would have the actual dominion over those subdued. We see this in the book of Revelation, where the emperor is presented as the "scarlet woman," and the one who made sure orders were carried out was pictured as the beast from the earth who was also the false prophet.

The definition of *subdue* is "to conquer and bring into subjection," but it also carries the meaning of "to tread down, subjugate, and violate." These words leave no doubt about God's aim for His creation. Man was to be the ruler. I do think there is a softer meaning in reference to the time when man would continue to learn the secrets of the universe so that his learning would make the universe work for him. Adam would have realized the depth of his responsibility from the definition of the Hebrew word. Anyone, by force of power or intrigue, can conquer, but there is more to the success of that goal than conquering.

This principle probably is also true of subduing the earth. Until the principles of the universe are useful to man, they are not yet subdued. I strongly suspect that the job of subduing the universe will never be complete, but I think it is awesome what man has learned and the various applications by which he has been able to make use of that knowledge.

Dominion would also indicate man's authority to use knowledge as he sees fit. This doesn't mean that his decisions are all good but that his "dominion over" allows his choice in the same way that God gives us *choice*. I see a subtle difference, both of which are important. MacArthur gives us this definition: "a productive ordering of the earth and its inhabitants to yield its riches and accomplish God's purposes."[9] I correlate this statement to what I see as the progressive nature of man's ability to *reason*. You would be perfectly correct in asking how I came to draw such a conclusion, as

---

7   Strong's Expanded Exhaustive Concordance, 1823.
8   Strong's Expanded Exhaustive Concordance, 7287.
9   John MacArthur, *MacArthur Bible Commentary* (Nashville: Thomas Nelson Publishers, 2005), 11.

I've gone outside of Scripture for information not found within. Here is my answer: We are able to know some things because of man's *reasoning ability, which was given by God.* Obviously, our conclusions are not always correct, but as we observe results, we are able to make changes in our conclusions and either start over or go from there.

I simply can't resist asking: of what does this remind you? Isn't this a carbon copy of the way we are allowed to learn God's will? What if the scientists who unravel these mysteries should say, "This is just too complicated, and I don't believe it can be done"? Exactly nothing would have been discovered. It is the same with us. Without reaching out for the possibilities, nothing is gained.

God created in such a way that man could "subdue" in incremental steps. So also is the path to Him. You can't learn it all at once, but you can take one step at a time as you continue to seek. God chose for it to be this way, and the key is to always continue to seek. It seems that He assembled knowledge in such a way that man could discern with the guidance of the Spirit in a piece-by-piece progressive method. In my mind, this also indicates that He created the universe by principles. (This is strictly an opinion.) I've no doubt that He could have created it without principles and commanded it to function, but it would seem that our God has no use for uselessness. Everything has a function—the sun, the moon, the stars, and even insects. They all work together for a purpose, and they seem always to demonstrate another principle that allows man's effort to move forward. It is a wise scientist (or anyone else) who is able to recognize and follow God's principles. Our function as His messengers is much the same as it is for scientists—we take one step at a time in an effort to remain within His framework. When we do, this we grow spiritually. Nothing is wasted. All things possess purpose, by which we need to honor and praise Him.

A vital part of any change that occurs is the matter of self-analysis, which can either lead to spiritual growth or in its absence, stagnancy. The need for knowledge continually grows which enables spiritual growth and changes you as you continue to feed your heart and your mind. I could give you a long list of understandings that have come to me, some with difficulty as I struggled with my intellect (the mind can definitely lead you astray) and at other times when understanding came in a "flash of understanding."[10] It was, as Tozer says, compatible with God's teaching, though not as previously understood by me. This means, pure and simple, that I took over from God when He was working with me. He is remarkable in that He is able to work with us from *where we are* at any stage in our development. Be absolutely sure that you don't allow your logic (or whatever you depend on) to fill you with confusion.

Examples of man's ability to think and reason and draw conclusions are everywhere. In the scientific world, such principles such as gravity, the workings of the universe and space, electricity, relativity, and the cellular system, including the atomic cell structure and DNA, have been discovered. The more we think about God, the more we will begin to feel Him, and it will be through this bonding of mind and spirit that He will begin to reveal to us the light of what we study. My word of advice: try really hard not to limit Him by what you currently know. Leave the door open for more knowledge and understanding, and at least a part of their function will unravel when God sees that you are ready for this particular information. This is the path of spiritual growth. Many other principles, as yet unknown to man's still-limited ability to learn, wait for the conclusions he might draw from them, either now or in the future.

In the days of Adam and the patriarchs, the things that were subdued were not quite as grand but were what was needed at the time. Such knowledge helped man learn how to plow, plant, and harvest and how to survive. Man always has been required to use his learned abilities to discern meanings and by doing so, he has combined the twin aspects of survival and thriving.

Another way in which man was created in God's likeness and in His image is in his ability to produce children in his own image and likeness. Although the two methods are different, given the spiritual/physical patterns, the outcome seems to be quite similar. In the physical realm, children's images resemble their parents' images, as God's children resemble Him in His essential characteristics, which would include both mind and spirit. In ways we do not begin to comprehend, this coincides with the receipt of DNA from parents/ancestors. As children of God,

---

[10] Tozer, *The Knowledge of the Holy,* 18.

this seemingly *different* quality may coincide with such attributes as the yearning for the Spirit and for communion with God.

These are the ways in which we are obviously created in God's image. Again, I suspect that I have only touched the surface, but I continue to learn and grow as I contemplate God's greatness in the realm of our likeness of His image.

My Motivation to Write

Why am I writing on this seldom-studied subject? Basically, it is because I am convinced that Satan has influenced the world to believe that God's new covenant is nothing more than a glorified rulebook. It was a brilliant ruse. Just like his approach with Eve, it gave a little truth mixed with a whole lot of lies, and like Eve, we didn't know how to counter the charge, because for the most part, we were totally ignorant of the old law and not extremely knowledgeable of the new. The result is that we fell for his line, just as Eve did. Now, if you remember, Eve suffered for not believing God, and I ask you: "Where does that leave us?"

Listen carefully: Christianity is not a matter of obeying a lot of rules for the sake of salvation. I can almost hear a thunderous roar of voices denying this premise as they reply, well, you couldn't prove it by me! This is why the foundation of every chapter will deal, to some extent, with this misconception. As I built both my premise and the conclusions to follow, and as I explored the content I wanted to cover, I became convinced that Satan—instead of attacking the idea of a Spirit who lives within, who guides the follower in his spiritual life, who comforts in time of sorrow and teaches how to possess God's nature—saw the advantage of emphasizing obedience rather than spirituality. Lying had always been of benefit to him, so his decision was to lie again, and it was easily accepted, because as he knew, man had always been expected to obey and had always been disobedient. It was an inspired moment for him and one that would earn for him many souls, and all he had to do was downplay the importance of spirituality and overemphasize the rule-book concept as the "real" Bible. He was more than familiar with the odious idea (to him) of obedience and knew it would strike a chord within the mind of man.

If you believe that being a follower of Christ is only a matter of laws—"Do this, but don't do that"—and that you know and obey most of the "important rules"; and if you also believe that you've never really committed any of the "big" sins so you are comfortable in the status of your salvation, then you most likely are not going to get much from this account that chronicles the life of the spiritual person.

Personally, I do not believe at all that Christianity is just about rules. If it were no more than rules, the church would not have survived throughout the centuries that have followed the crucifixion and resurrection of our Lord. Satan's misrepresentation of Christianity, however, does have a bearing on why the church becomes stymied in its growth. In order to identify the roadblock, we must be able to recognize its true nature and the resulting damage it has caused, along with ridding ourselves of all of its implications. Rule-following is not the real problem; it is attitude. Our hearts are sick. Too often, we resent being told anything, really. We want to do it our way, whatever "it" is. We have yet to be exposed, in its fullest sense, to God's *nature*, of which we know little, or we would already be at work to achieve this for our Lord, who has done so much for us. Consequently, we suffer, but more importantly, God's message suffers. We are truly heartsick. In order to resolve this nearly fatal "heart attack," we must begin immediately to seek within ourselves and in Scripture, to learn just how we can remedy what has become a crisis. We must do away with the idea that our lives are shored up by rules that are at best out-of-date and at worst confining in their nature. Legalism and rule-following was an attitude condemned by Jesus. Of utmost importance, however, is the truth that following Jesus is a matter of the heart and that our desire is to please Jesus and through Him, God the Father. It will only be by means of an attitude of love for Him and for those who do not know Him that we seek to commit ourselves to the Lord's service. Through this love for Jesus, we are guided in the direction of true spiritual growth by the one who knows God and His Son; that is, the Holy Spirit. Yes, the same Spirit who dwells within your heart, the Holy Spirit of God. Love is the challenge before us.

As Christians in this period of history (perhaps in all periods), we have done a very poor job of loving the Lord with our hearts, minds, and souls, which produces in us a desire to follow biblical concepts and principles. Although some do, they are a minority of those who claim to be Christians around the world. This, my friends, is the reason we do not convert those in the world to spiritual living. The world sees us and knows what we truly are, so others don't believe us when we preach Jesus. They laugh, or they ridicule. This is a book about renewal, not conversion, but the principles for success in the two are much the same. It is through our love for Him that belief is made genuine to those around us. Lives are then so renewed that the changes wrought by the Spirit reveal our Lord to mankind. I am sorry to express the opinion that the gift of God's Spirit is largely a gift that is unrecognized and underutilized. The desperate desire to become like Him is the crisis we are facing. It requires a *decision* for change, *devotion* to the one who died for us and a genuine *self-discipline* in order to be successful.

1

Following the Heart of Jesus

Love—Love—Love

Let me tell you what following Jesus, the Christ, is all about. The most important aspect is love. When the creation was in God's mind alone, before the foundation of the world, as He developed the plan, there was love.

Now let me ask a question: have you ever planned a house, a garden, or a child? It is done with loving care. No detail is too small to consider. That's the way it was with our God. How do I know this? I know it because of His love that I see all around me; these are the aftereffects, the glow of His love in what He created for you and me. He didn't have to make it beautiful, but He did. It is impossible not to see His love as it surrounds me, yet as hard as I try to perpetuate that beauty in the world around me, my efforts cannot be compared with His.

We were designed with the ultimate purpose of being in fellowship with Him. The plan was that we would *choose* to follow Him because we love Him, so He gave us the principle of choice. Choice enables love, but let me tell you something you may not know: it also enables evil, because evil is very convenient to choose, and Satan makes it sound like fun.

Why, then, didn't God just do it another way? It is a good question, but there was only one other way it could have been done, and it was not what God wanted. Had He ordained that man *had* to obey, there would have been no love in the transaction, only a command to do as you are told. Man would have been similar to a robot. Would he have loved God? I think not.

You may wonder, then, "But why evil?" My answer would be that evil is the opposite of good. There was no other choice. But where did evil come from, and where does evil abide? Is it in heaven with God? It is absolutely *not* in heaven with God, because it is impossible for good and evil to dwell together. God is light, and evil is darkness. Think about it. As the sun leaves where it has spent the day and moves about the hemisphere, darkness follows. Darkness doesn't get too close to the sun, or the rays of heat would penetrate its substance, causing it to disappear. Light does away with what it can't see. Darkness hides what it doesn't want you to see.

Where did evil come from, where does it abide, and did God create evil? In my opinion, God did not create evil. If you believe as I do, that leaves only one other option: evil has always been, just as God has always been. In that case, it may have been logical that the difference between good and evil was the choice man would be given. I must forewarn you, however, that God cautions us against pitting our human logic against His knowledge. According to Tozer, "The believing heart confesses without proof; to obtain proof admits doubt and is superfluous."[11] In case you are not familiar with Mr. Tozer, he was an American pastor, preacher, author, editor, and spiritual mentor. Born into poverty and self-educated, he published fourteen books, and authored more than forty, with many others attributed to him. He had two honorary doctorates, and two of his books are considered classics. Of contemporary Christianity, he feared the church was following a dangerous course toward "worldly" concerns. Prayer was a vital necessity in his life and was reflected in his writings and was, indeed, a definition of the man. He died in 1963 at the age of sixty-six.[12]

God does not show partiality, and it is evident that those who choose wickedness draw away from God as they follow Satan's guide. Wickedness simmers as loyalties are drawn by lies devised by the grandeur of Satan's imagination. Though we have no certain knowledge of when the angels were granted choice, we know they were by the secrecy of God's plan and the division of loyalty among the angels as they listened to and followed

---

[11] Tozer, *The Knowledge of the Holy*, 18.
[12] A. W. Tozer, Wikipedia.

Satan. He was unable to lead away all of the angels of the heavenly host, but imagine the pain it must have caused God to lose any of them. Revelation called it a third, although numbers in Revelation are not literal. In this case, I believe the number represents not a small number but not the entire host (Revelation 12:4). Lest we become indignant that even *some* of the angels could desert Him, let me remind you who in today's world enables Satan in his work: no other than you and I. Satan *cannot* force us to do his will, or he would. God, on the other hand, *could force us* but does not. The two statements are worlds apart, and therein is the truth of good and evil.

Some think that the world and the universe were created prior to Satan's creation. I don't know that it matters, except to know that he was created before man was created. We often hear the phrase, "when time shall be no more," and similar phrases, such as, "at the end of time." To me, it is a comforting thought to know that our lives in heaven will not be guided by checking the clock. We do know that God's plan for reconciliation was prepared before the foundation of the world (Ephesians 1:3–6), and though we have no information regarding the immediate time in which Satan was created, we do have constant evidence of the damage of his rebellion on earth, with Adam and Eve in the garden, followed by Cain and Abel, then Noah and the flood, and then Job, to name only a few. A careful reading of both the Old and New Testaments reveals Satan's constant insubordination and interference in the progression of God's plan.

Don't make the mistake of feeling pity for Satan. He wasn't forced to follow the path he chose. Although God knew that someone would rise up to be the leader of the rebellion, it is important to understand that Satan was not created for that purpose. Out of God's omniscience, however, He would have known that Satan would be the one.

I have always wondered how long Adam and Eve were in the garden before Satan made his seemingly innocuous announcement that God didn't really mean they couldn't eat the fruit of the Tree of Life; they just had misunderstood Him. The expulsion from the garden was the immediate consequence with which they had to deal, but as we know, the ultimate consequence was the crucified Son of God and a war between God and Satan, which eventually was refocused on a war between man and Satan. This is the war that continues to this day.

3

As a result of man's decision to believe Satan's lie instead of the truth, all mankind has had the same decision to make, over and over again. It is an individual decision for an unchanging hypothesis. As a result, man lost his relationship with God, not because of a lack of God's love but because of man's decision not to believe in God and His love. God's hatred[13] for sin resulted in mankind's expulsion from the garden, because light cannot dwell with darkness. Many do not understand that if there was no 'salvation from the wrath of God' there would be no salvation from sin.' I've gone to the dictionary to see what our modern word experts have to say about anger and wrath.

Beginning with the word 'wrath' we learn that its definition is to experience intense anger and indignation or strong antagonism and resentful displeasure that comes from a *sense of injury*. Such a rejection of redemption for *self* is enough to precipitate God's anger and then there is the rejection of His Son who endured great pain and anguish in the purchase of the gift. Can we really wonder at the indignation, the displeasure, the resentment against such a one who cannot even love himself? One who can reject the Son not only is lacking in love, he/she has no concept of justice which will prevail at the time of judgment.

Some consider it unworthy of our Lord to even express anger yet one of the most striking characteristics of the Bible is the vigor with which both testaments emphasize the reality and terror of God's wrath. One might even say that the point is labored in that "more references are to be found in a concordance regarding God's anger and wrath than there is to love and tenderness."

God provided for the certainty that sin would enter the hearts of His human creation by preparing for a foundation that would be built upon the prophets of Old Testament history and upon the apostles of New Testament history, of which Jesus, the Christ would be the crowning glory. The foundation began with the expulsion from the garden, the curse on the serpent, and a changed life from the beauty and joy of living and caring for the garden to learning to live in a world that now included sin. All of the foundation would lead to a church in which Christ would be the head

---

[13] J. I. Packer, *Knowing God, With Study Guide,* 20th Anniversary Ed., copyright 1973 by J. I. Packer, Americanized and retyped 1993, publisher Inter Varsity Press, with permission of Hodda and Stroughton, Limited, London, 149

and the means through which forgiveness would at last be available to the people. Released from the bondage of the Law, to the freedom of choice, man would still have consequences for the choices made, eternal life or eternal death. Its' most marvelous attribute would be the cleansing of sin that would apply not only to new believers but to all past believers who had lived their lives in faith of the promise. The requirements for such forgiveness would be mercy on God's part, and repentance on man's part. The foundation would be complete with the resurrection and ascension of Jesus and would actually be for both man and God in that it would be a 'bringing together' (a propitiation) by appeasement for sin. I know we don't usually say it that way, but the plan would actually be for both man and God, in that it brought the offender (man) and the offended (God) back into contact with each other, achieving reconciliation. This, my friend is the extent of God's love for man.

There are many who fail to grasp the significance of this principle in regard to God's anger and His wrath, but the simple truth is that we must understand God's wrath or we cannot understand the gospel of salvation from wrath. It is all about justice where 'wrath' is the word of retribution for unbelievers in order to balance the scales of justice. One must keep in mind that unbelievers chose their path just as believers chose theirs. Without justice of what benefit would any of it be? Toward that end, God continued to teach the message of love because that was the key to all that would follow.

The apostle John has always summed up such messages of love in the very best way, but of course his message was not available for many centuries.

> Beloved let us love one another, for love is from God; and everyone who loves is born of God and knows God. The one who does not love does not know God, for God is love. By the love of God was manifested in us that God has sent His only begotten Son into the world so that we might live through Him. In this is love, not that we loved God, but that He loved us and sent His Son to be the *propitiation* [justification] for our sins. Beloved, if God so loved us, we also ought to love one another. No one has

seen God at any time; if we love one another, God abides in us, and *His love is perfected in us.* By this we know that we abide in Him and He abides in us, because He has given us of His Spirit. (1 John 4:7–11 NASB).

To reemphasize this love factor I have gone back to the Old Testament to illustrate the continuity of God's plan for man, in that the core of teaching in the old was based on love. To illustrate in abbreviated form, the following points provide the heart or, if you please, the meaning of Christianity, some from the old, others from the new: I call these the non-negotiable commands, because they have been with us throughout both covenants. Please notice that each stems from the presence of love.)

- *Love the Lord your God with all your heart, soul, and mind* Deuteronomy 6:5. (God is love. We cannot expect to know Him or emulate Him without love.)
- *Have no other gods besides (before) the Lord God* Exodus 20:3-5. (This is protection for us, but it is also because He is a jealous God. He is jealous of those who are put before Him in importance. He is jealous of the wickedness we hide within our hearts when we have already given ourselves to Him.)
- *Love others as you love yourself* Leviticus 19:18, First Corinthians 13:13. (This is both motivation and protection. Please note that it is important to love yourself, not obsessively or egotistically but as belonging to God, which indicates both assistance for those in need and respect for individuals, God's children.)
- *Repent of your sins* Matthew 16:12, 14-15, Second Peter 3:14. (This demonstrates the humility of your heart and your submission to the Father as well as your desire for salvation, which will keep you prepared, ready for the coming of the Lord.)
- *Believe in His incarnation, His crucifixion, His resurrection and His ascension* John 8:32, John 14:6, John 16:13. (These are the elementary truths of salvation. Can you believe them and accept them as the truths they are? If you can, it will put you in touch with the reconciliation of God's grace. This is what propitiation is all about.

- *Believe in the atoning blood of Jesus which paid the debt for your sin and mine* Romans 5:9, Ephesians 1:7, Hebrews 9:22. (This brings grace and the gift of the Spirit as well as forgiveness to each believer.)

These are the principles of Christianity. They are not in themselves laws, they are a path. Make no mistake God *wants* all people to obey these principles because they are for our benefit, both immediately and in eternity, but He cut us an awful lot of slack. Have you ever thought about that? He knows that even when we try our very best, we will make mistakes, because we are human. As a result, we are judged by what our heart intends. That might not work with you or with me at the helm, but God is different. He knows what is in the heart, and He makes no mistakes. Consider that in thanksgiving and gratitude, and then give Him your best. I promise you that He will accept it.

A Review of the Law

In addition to preparing for the nation that Israel would be eventually, God gave them the Law. This was given at Mount Sinai as the Israelites made their journey from captivity in Egypt to the country that had been prepared for them, Canaan. I hope you realize that the Canaanites were not just arbitrarily thrown out of their country. Their removal was because of their immorality. They worshiped idols, contrary to God's instructions, and practiced immorality in their daily lives. They had been given many years in which to repent and turn from their wickedness, but they chose not to do that, so this episode demonstrates the *consequences* of their decision.

The Law replaced the patriarchal method of communication with man, in part *probably* because of population growth in the world but also because it was a part of God's plan. Communication of the Law was done by means of the priesthood, rather than through the patriarchs. The Law had three purposes: (1) no one would be justified by the works of the Law, for by the Law is the *knowledge* of sin (Romans 3:20); (2) the superiority of God's righteousness in comparison to man's sin's (Romans 3:19–26;

Romans 7:12; (3) each of the verses listed lead to the third purpose (reason) which was the coming of Christ (Galatians 3:24–25).

Paul has simply said that God knew there was a problem here, because we don't always know that we are sinning, so here is what God did for us. The priests received the message from the high priests, (who had received it from God) and passed it on to the people. How does it work today? Paul said we are "justified by His grace as a gift through Jesus Christ" (Romans 3:24) "whom God displayed publicly as a propitiation" (on the cross) "to demonstrate His (God's) righteousness" because "in the forbearance (patience) of God, He passed over the sins previously committed" (sins under the law and previous to the law); for the demonstration of His righteousness at the present time". (He possesses no partiality between the two groups of old and new, (Romans 2:11), so that He would be just and the justifier of the one who has faith in Jesus" ("just" to those who lived before the crucifixion and resurrection and "the justifier" of those who lived following these events).

You may question why we introduce this brief review of the Law. The Law is the "forerunner" of the Christian Church and can, in many ways, help us to understand this "new transaction" God has created for our benefit. Actually, to think of it as new is slightly misleading, because it is more correctly the final touches of His plan for regaining fellowship with man, who sins. In the same way that agreements or contracts must be legal in our world, God considered legality of importance in His covenants with man. Each covenant has been verified and sealed with information of importance, which included incentives for man to be obedient but also, perhaps, just because God wanted man to know the benefits the contract provided.

You should recognize a few more things that will lend validity to the similarities between the two covenants. The surprise is that while the Mosaic Law was a law of rules that were both severe in application and in the punishment that followed, the principles involved were a matter of teaching, just like a parent teaches a child for the purpose of benefiting the child's understanding. Those lessons were out of the way—meaning they were set aside, whether learned or not learned by the time the Law ended (Romans 10:4)—but they are referred to in Scripture as *fulfilled* (Galatians 5:14), in order that a new and better covenant could go into effect. This is the covenant under which we live and breathe and hopefully grow in praise of the Creator. God's principles did not change. Basically, what happened was that the old Law taught but the new law taught as it made application. They are connected in many ways that have to do with growing in spirituality, but the keeping of the Law (the rules) has been replaced with the new commandments of love and the ability to choose. This places the responsibility on man, rather than on God. It is necessary to keep that in mind as you study, so that it will be easier to comprehend the connection between the two covenants. We will share later in the study some of the specifics of the differences between the two.

The Israelites were originally called the Hebrews. Later, they were called Israelites, after one of Abraham's grandsons (Jacob, the twin brother of Esau). After the battle Jacob fought in his sleep with God, God changed his name from Jacob to Israel, and the twelve tribes of Israel were thereafter called Israelites. Much later, Jacob's name was corrupted to the word Jew, and this became another name by which the Israelites are known. In the same manner, God also refers to Christians as Israel (Romans 9:6, 30; Galatians 6:16). This is a perfect illustration of our oneness in God.

I see the presentation that Christianity is a rulebook as a clever idea of Satan's. His grossly inaccurate interpretation of being a Christian has made us complacent, without enthusiasm, and extremely passive. Hopefully, if enough attention shines upon this lie, we will make some progress in spiritual growth, which I hope will bear a similarity to the enthusiasm that surrounded the beginning of the church at Pentecost.

All of these happenings occurred during the building of the foundation and are still very connected to what God is doing toward His ultimate goal.

2

The Need for Spirituality

Leaving Elementary Principles

The writer of Hebrews exhorted the Christian Jews to leave the "discussion of the elementary principles of Christ," and "let us go on to perfection, not laying again the foundation of repentance from dead works and of faith toward God" (Hebrews 6:1). What is he saying? For the purpose of understanding, let's take a look at forgiveness from the standpoint of the "elementary principles" to which he refers. Our understanding that we have been granted forgiveness of sin because of Christ's atoning blood means we are ready to move past that knowledge of how it works and learn other things we can do that will show our dedication to carrying out the Great Commission.

We understand that forgiveness has not yet reached all people of the world, and it must continue to be taught, along with its connection to baptism and the Holy Spirit, but it is also imperative that those already in Christ experience the knowledge of God's nature and seek to make it their own, in order that their lives reflect His great light. This is spiritual growth.

While we do not forget the importance of the first gift, we must, of necessity, move forward as we pursue the righteousness designed for those who are within the body. It is time for more substantial "food." If you have experienced the dietary needs of an infant, you understand exactly what the writer of Hebrews is saying. An infant won't continue to grow in a satisfactory manner unless he moves forward from milk and pabulum. It is the same for us as Christians. We must tackle the more difficult things that God has for us in order to grow. The writer calls this "going on to perfection" (Hebrews 6:1). What, then, is perfection?

Perfection is a word used in Scripture to mean "complete." We are complete in Christ Jesus when we finish the course of physical life with our faith intact. The significance of the word "perfection" in its normal definition means "without imperfections," and we realize immediately that only God fits this definition. Man in his natural state is not perfect. Paul tells us, however, that we preach Jesus and His having been crucified for the purpose of "teaching every man in all wisdom, *that we may present every man perfect in Christ Jesus*" (emphasis mine Colossians 1:28). So, even though we are not perfect in and of ourselves, we can be perfect in Jesus. He continues by saying that it is the wisdom of that which is taught (the atoning blood of Jesus) that makes it possible for Jesus to present us to the Father, who grants us of His own perfection, providing that we have kept the faith and finished the course (1 Timothy 6:12). This resembles the manner in which our sins are forgiven, in that God views us in the purity of the One who gave His blood. It would seem that our debt to the Father continues to grow.

A Few Good Rules

Although living for Christ is not a matter of following rules, a few rules have been held over from those given at Sinai. Normally called (a part of) the Ten Commandments, they are rich in many ways. Yes, they were rules, and they are still rules. (The abbreviated list precedes chapter 2 if you need to review.) See if you can figure out why they are so important. My curious mind decided long ago that they were information for a happy and productive life, and I was amazed that God considered our lives instead of His own in making these rules. Look at them carefully.

Worshiping only God prevents your falling away into idolatry and evil; love of others keeps you from loving yourself too much, allowing you to get along with others. Loving God creates devotion and the desire to please Him and provides strength for self-discipline. How many more reasons can you list for their importance? The last three laws come from the new covenant. Repentance is the condition by which forgiveness is granted, and belief in Jesus is the only way to God. These commands are not for God's benefit; they are for man's benefit. They are fundamental issues. I call them the non-negotiable rules. There is no room to maneuver out of obedience and still be satisfactory with God.

Let me add a postscript to the last paragraph. As with all teaching that comes from God, we must understand that this is what *we* know of God's revealed word. He will always teach using means that are beneficial for the learner because of His love for us individually. It therefore should create in each of us an occasion for awe. We need to rejoice if one is saved by methods unknown to us. An example I think of is the thief who hung on the cross by Jesus and condemned the other man for his lack of respect for God, commenting that Jesus had done nothing to deserve punishment. While the new covenant was not yet in effect, and there is no indication that the thief had followed the law, Jesus' comment indicates that the man would be with Him in paradise. The conclusion seems to be that this man's heart was all he had to offer, and like the widow's mite, it was all he had, was given freely, and was therefore accepted.

God's message repeats over and over the importance of the heart in all that we do and all that we think. I hope we grasp from this incident of the thief on the cross the importance of the heart in our relationship with God and others. Our understanding of God's acceptance of the thief reveals that His heart is filled with compassion.

The conclusions we may draw (after the fact) seem to be that the thief had a compassionate heart, even in the circumstances in which he found himself. There may have been other reasons why he wound up on a cross next to Jesus, but we have no way of knowing, though God knows, and it was His decision to bless him. I believe that while we should not question His decision, we are allowed to use His compassion as an example to add to our goal to be like Him.

What lesson might we learn from the other thief? It is obvious that either because of or in spite of his situation, he didn't have the desire to make a plea for Jesus. He wasn't interested in anyone's situation except his own; thus, he displayed a cold and ruthless heart. He reminds me of those who don't care when someone else hurts because the pain is not their own.

Even this drastic situation could not change such a cold heart, because it is hardened to the point of being dead.

Do you understand that despite circumstances, if you love God, you will obey His voice? We either believe or we don't. We either experience God's sorrow over the persecution and death of His Son, who took our place on that cross, or we don't. By the same token, we either experience the sorrow that God feels for our own disobedience, or we don't. If we feel such sorrow, we will repent of our own transgressions. Choice is not granted regarding the non-negotiable commands. All other laws seem to be a matter of choice. In our efforts to be obedient, we may deny our Creator a relationship with us, saying to ourselves, "I'll think about it tomorrow." Perhaps, then, in defense for what was just said, we would offer our futile reasoning. "I go to services," you might say. "I get the children to classes, and I give," and all of that is good, but it isn't necessarily the *feeding of the soul* that develops a personal relationship with our Father and leads to spiritual growth. Unfortunately, it is the habit of our lives and seems many times to be truthfully all we can manage. I am asking that we reexamine and, if necessary, "overhaul" the specifics of our lives so that a relationship with the Lord can belong to each of us. When we are able to rid our lives of clutter, the results can be amazing.

Time, Priorities and Decisions

Quiet times of meditation with the Lord are a requirement for our spiritual growth. Anyone engaged in a school curriculum or a training course has experienced the need to contemplate the knowledge gained, the trajectory of a chosen career path, and the wisdom of the material to be learned. So why do we fail to see that the same dedication of self is needed to grow spiritually? The crunch for time to get everything done was perhaps not a problem originally in our lives, but as time accumulates additional responsibilities, our obligation to God suddenly takes a backseat. As God is supposed to be first in our priorities, this means that we are giving Him our leftovers and cheating ourselves out of an enriching and loving relationship in a world that is desperate for love.

Do we realize what we are doing? I doubt that we do, because we look at it as if we have no choice, saying, "I do what *has* to be done." We do a lot of things in ignorance, but it is well to remember that God no longer accepts ignorance as an excuse for lack of any kind. His demand has always been that we give Him the best that is in us. If we compare what we give Him with His requirement for the condition of the animals that were to be sacrificed or the offerings that were made to Him, we can see the difference. Animals were to be without spot or blemish—young, healthy, the best of the flock. The offerings from the harvest were to be the best that was produced. These requirements do not sound as if they were the things that were left over. I confess to you that I don't know if our sacrifice of self is accepted when we give Him what is left of our time. Sadly, both God and mankind lose.

Remember the widow and her "two mites" (amounting to only about a penny in our culture), whose gift was considered the greatest of the day? It was all she had, but that isn't why it was the greatest. It was the greatest because she gave it willingly with all of her heart. This demonstrates an incredible example of love and faith, (Mark 12:41–44). Such love for God is phenomenal.

The decision to grow and the commitment to grow spiritually are on the order of the ones we made when we gave ourselves to Jesus, asking that He become the Lord of our lives, the head, the one to whom we belong in all things. There is a healing process in the commitment alone that takes us past the passivity we have come to accept. We do not forget the first principles to which we are so indebted, but *there is a renewal of enthusiasm and excitement* as we begin to realize that the Lord has so much more for us than we can imagine. As we renew our thanksgiving and reexamine our hope, I encourage you to have as your guiding light the statement of the father of a demon-possessed child. When asked by the Lord if he believed, his answer was, "Lord, I believe; help my unbelief!" (Mark 9:24). So must it be with us: "Lord, help our unbelief!"

Decisions are life changers; whims are not. As we review our track record, from the time of our spiritual birth to now, we can perhaps gain some perspective to use in our life in the service of our Lord, as we aspire to move forward at this time. Are we preaching and teaching the gospel daily because of the way we live, move, and speak? Are we converting the spiritually blind by the image we portray, or have we taken over God's plan of how salvation must be achieved and then substituted our own? I would urge parents to recognize that after their responsibility to God, the family comes next. I do realize that the breadwinner of the family has specific duties and time frames, but I would still affirm that the primary responsibility is to the family. This can take many forms, especially in caring for children, with many resolutions that fit the needs of your family. I would remind you that this responsibility to family is to your "first people," for whom you are personally responsible to teach the gospel, and in some ways, it can be the most difficult.

Many activities seem worthy of your time, but weigh their worth with the relationship-building needs of your family, both with God and each other. This includes those activities that a well-meaning church provides. Don't feel guilty when you decide that time with family is of more importance than a scheduled event, either of a secular or religious nature. My advice is to consider your circumstances and make your decision in wisdom and prayer. It takes time, prayer, study, and meditation to establish the inner qualities of God. Strive to establish yours, and the legacy of faith in our Father will be an inspiration to others. There are so many ways in which we may serve Him, as Paul indicates in 1 Corinthians 12. Our service is dictated by the abilities God has given and must therefore be respected. We are not carbon copies of each other but unique, as God created us. Our timing on the Lord's continuum will never be the same as it will be for anyone else, so this is a wonderful time to remember being submissive to each other. Each of us must strive to find and follow the schedule that God has for us, without comparing what we accomplish (or fail to accomplish) with what others are able to do or not do. Remember, the heart is the mother lode from which spirituality evolves.

As we commit to spiritual growth, we admit to a certain amount of fear that we may not be able to understand the guidance of the Spirit. This is not fear of the Spirit but fear of our own inadequacy. Unspoken words are so easily misunderstood, and perhaps we have known others who have traveled this path for various reasons, other than spiritual growth. I would suggest that there is only one way that we can fail in this endeavor, and that is if we fail to try, and to try, we have to start. A measure of the

Spirit is already within us; we have only to begin. He waits patiently for our awakening to His presence. We must become as aware of Him as we (hopefully) are aware of the Father and the Son. It is only by beginning that we can make progress in correcting our spiritual nature.

3

The Inner Man

Self–Improvement

When I speak of self-improvement, I speak of the inner self, the person within. This is where our growth must originate. Even a quick scan of the gospels demonstrates that a lot of what Jesus taught in regard to spirituality involved the transfer of religious worship from the external to the internal. You might say that worship of that day had a lot of symbolic meaning, and to an extent that was true. But had the priests (and later, the rabbis) who represented the sects understood what Jesus was teaching, they would not have become so completely external; it would also have had its spiritual interpretation. The Jews thought their righteousness would evolve from what could be accomplished externally, while Jesus was teaching that the motivation of the heart was the source of righteousness. The core of such motivation was the teaching of love. Activity that came from loving God was acceptable because it loved Him— *not because it was a part of the law* but because they wanted to *serve God.*

So it is with us today. *Internal motivation describes worship that is embedded in the heart.* This is the goal that we seek in accordance with God's statement of so long ago: "I will put my laws in their mind and write them on their hearts; and I will be their God, and they shall be my people" (Hebrews 8:10). This reveals it as God's goal as well. The psalmist said, "Your word I have treasured in my heart that I may not sin against you" (Psalm 119:11 NASB). What a beautiful testimony to God's plan. I don't think I ever considered this idea as a protection against sin, but of course, it makes sense, doesn't it? "In my heart" seems to indicate possession of knowledge, and the consideration for what it has to say and "location within the heart" speaks of its value and importance to us.

Paul's statement in this regard is more than a little frightening when we consider that we can slip away from God without knowing what is happening, even as the Israelites did, when we fail to "pursue righteousness by faith." We speak here of an active, believing faith and are told to pursue it. Does that have the sound of passivity? An active, growing faith "pursues the righteousness of God's nature." Only then will we begin to know Him. Only then will we begin to possess some of the righteousness to which the Spirit's guidance takes us.

In God's long period of silence in the time between the covenants, it seems that the leaders of the Israelites began to take advantage of His silence and started building their own kingdoms. Things were mixed up and probably somewhat confusing with the dissension between the leaders, and they began to take things into their own hands. In part, this meant that those who had power used it to enforce their interpretations of the laws, and it also meant that those who had power jealously guarded it. Perhaps the most damaging problem, however, was that *they were divided* in their following of the Lord. God tells us that there was still a believing remnant, and it was to the remnant that Jesus directed His message when He began His ministry. Evidence of this is in our Lord's explanation to His apostles of why He always spoke in parables. "To you it has been granted to know the mysteries of the kingdom of God, but to the rest it is in parables, so that seeing they may not see, and hearing they may not understand" (Luke 8:9 NASB). Those of whom He spoke didn't want knowledge; they wanted to argue as a means of maintaining their power. This is a good point for us to remember.

Obedience

The preceding verses indicate the need for obedience of all things learned by faith. *That there is always the possibility of getting it wrong only emphasizes the value of doing by faith.* If we obey in faith, we've done the best we can, and God is able to pick up our pieces. If, on the other hand, we use our own human interpretations, without acknowledging God's omnipotence, omniscience, and omnipresence, we are misleading those around us and are creating division.

The Gentiles obeyed the message for which God had sent Paul to them and promptly utilized it in their lives, which demonstrated their belief in what they had heard. The Jews who had long anticipated the coming of the Messiah rejected the message, because it was in conflict with their interpretation of its meaning. Paul was saying, "You are to 'do' it because you believe, not because a law says you have to." Although we will examine motivation a bit later, I didn't want you to miss this extraordinary illustration of how faith can be corrupted. For now, let's move on to the significance of obedience.

I am convinced that we have lost something in regard to our obedience. We began our lives in Christ with excitement, perhaps a little fear, and quite a lot of self-consciousness—or at least I did, perhaps because I was so young. The fear is that we will make mistakes, and of course we will; God even expects it. While living for Him is a process, and we learn the process gradually, we do need to learn new ways of teaching progression without losing enthusiasm or momentum. Baptism as a beginning is an event to be cherished, but it is still a beginning. So much remains to be done.

Asking for prayers to hold you up before God, as you learn the process of living for Him, is essential, both in a private and a group setting. Details of exactly why you need prayers are not essential publicly. Your private prayers are beneficial in that they will keep you in constant communication with the Father as you strive to learn and grow spiritually. The change in you and the growth that occurs is diametrically opposed to what Satan wants and is a battle fought on two fronts as your ever-strengthened spirit goes against both Satan and you.

Don't try to resolve everything at once. Decide on your priority and a plan of attack. This is what comes next, after baptism. Count on your Bible for information instead of on friends, preachers, or relatives. Shared information, at this point, is an invitation to gather false information. Wait until you are a bit stronger and know how to affirm or deny within your heart what someone tells you.

Obedience means that I have completely placed my trust in the atoning blood of Jesus Christ. At that moment, obedience is met by the delight of the supernatural grace of God and by the rejoicing of angels. This atonement is sometimes what we call "at-one-ment," meaning that the sacrifice of His blood, plus the submission of my will to His, has reconciled my desire to His desire for me, making us *one* in motivation and will. This is how atonement works for each individual who believes.

Seeking

One of the keys to spirituality is that we must never quit seeking. We are aided by the Spirit as we seek, and where the Spirit remains our teacher and our guide, we will begin to have that change in us for which we hope. Man has been given the responsibility of preaching the gospel, but granting the gift of the Spirit belongs to God. Isn't it logical, then, that we should teach and learn all we can learn regarding the virtues of the godly nature and the fruits that will show that nature, while remembering that the best lessons are those that are *seen*? Then, as each person pursues righteousness by means of the talents God has granted, that person will still be on his or her own continuum. Don't ever expect everyone to be identical. It just doesn't happen. The tools we've identified will help you as you struggle to get started. They will help you to utilize the gift God has so lovingly granted as He guides you into the truths you need to know.

We often fail to realize that God doesn't tell us all there is to know about anything, but He does tell us what we *need* to know. It is comforting to know that He cannot lie or make mistakes (Hebrews 6:18), and that the truth He teaches us is not myth (Isaiah 55:8–9; 1 Corinthians 13:12). One might say that He reveals Himself progressively but never erroneously. For this reason, it is an interesting fact that *God accepts the seeking heart where it is.* You do not have to know as much as someone else knows or wait as long to obey as someone else did, for God welcomes you from where you are, with the knowledge you possess. A good example is the thief on the cross. Unfortunately, the reasons for procrastination instead of obeying work together to strengthen the resistance we harbor as a "right" to do as we please. And this is absolutely true. We do have that right. It is God-given, but this does not mean it is the choice God wants us to make. So how are we to differentiate between following rules and making choices, and differentiate between what He allows and what He wants? I am convinced that the only way is to know the Spirit within, and heed His guidance.

It is important to understand that you will not know everything at once. Listen to your heart as you make decisions, and have the conviction that the Spirit will guide you. It is only then that you will be able to know that all situations are not alike. Basically this means that you follow the path of *internalizing* your faith. Those ways in which you discover your faith to be external instead of internal require your attention and your effort to make it a vital part of yourself. I hope that some of the following messages will be ways in which you may accomplish your goals.

If you are unsure of any action, ask yourself, "Where is the test of atonement in this situation?" You will know immediately the course of action by which the Spirit is directing you. "Would He be here with me? Would He do this?" It is an infallible test, a way that the Spirit can speak to you. "The natural man does not receive the things of the Spirit of God, for they are foolishness to him; nor can he know them, because they are spiritually discerned" (1 Corinthians 2:14). This says that *we cannot know God with the intellect* but only with the heart, by means of the Holy Spirit. It is impossible for us to know the mind of God, except by the Holy Spirit, who searches the "deep things of God" (1 Corinthians 2:10), and "in wisdom speaks of what He knows, ordained before the ages for our glory" (1 Corinthians 2:6–7).

Ignorance

The transition from the old covenant to the new covenant is seldom taught, but it is necessary in order to understand much of the new. Since it is a transition, I want to point out a law that could easily be overlooked. This law is with regard to ignorance. Under the Law that is often called the Law of Moses, God forgave the sin of ignorance. Understand that this was done in the same way other sins were handled under the Law, by a sacrificial offering once a year for "sins committed in ignorance." Animal blood was shed, plus a substitute goat was released into the wilderness as a symbol of Christ, who carried the sins of the people upon Himself but who would live after the resurrection. (As the lamb is the symbol of Jesus, the goat throughout the Bible is the symbol of sin.) This was God's method of keeping before the Israelites their hope for forgiveness that would come through the expected Messiah. After that event, the substitute would no longer be needed, nor would the yearly sacrifice be needed, because Jesus, the Lamb of God, would be the sacrifice one time for the sins of the world. This is what is referred to as a foreshadowing of what was to come.

When the Law changed, God no longer saw the necessity of allowing ignorance as an excuse for sin and today requires "that all men repent" (Acts 2:38). Forgiveness for ignorance may have existed prior to the Law, but as far as I know, there is no information that it did. I point this out because it is important to recognize that lots of things "were," of which we have not been informed. I find no mention of this rule regarding ignorance prior to the giving of the Law, but that doesn't mean it wasn't a part of God's plan at that time. I want to emphasize that God has all power, all knowledge, and is in all time periods. We simply cannot place Him in a box in our minds and think that because we have a certain understanding of Him, our understanding is complete. God is awesome and much greater than our minds can conceive.

Even Paul, who had boasted of his all-but-perfect Jewishness, was beneficiary of the law of ignorance. He said, "I was formerly a blasphemer, a persecutor, and an insolent man; but I obtained mercy because I did it ignorantly in unbelief" (1 Timothy 1:13). This poses an interesting concept; until Paul's conversion on the road to Damascus, he was still under the Law, and there was no forgiveness under the Law, except by looking forward in faith to the advent of the Messiah. I don't grasp all the ramifications of that for us today, but I do know that in Romans, we are told that if we sin under the Law, we will be judged by the Law. Faith in the promise was the criterion for judgment. There is another point that this verse fails to explain, and that is that Paul worshiped God; his heart's desire was to please God. I believe this is also a factor in his forgiveness. Compare the difference of a situation in which the one needing forgiveness had no use for God (someone like Satan).

There is a big difference between being told to do, and being given a choice between doing and not doing. What if I said, for instance, that you were required to wash up and pray before you eat? That would mean this is a law and is required. On the other hand, I could say, "In light of the importance of cleanliness and our need to be grateful for the food we are to eat, it would be good if you washed and then praised God for providing your food and thanked Him for caring for your physical body." That is a choice. The responsibility to respond is an individual matter. The one who chooses to follow the path of the suggestion to wash and pray will build some character and will begin to gain some understanding in regard to spirituality. The one who declines might have done as suggested and been resentful, or he could have been resentful because the suggestion was made and then declined. *God wants obedient believers who are cheerful.* This is one example of the difference between law and choice. Neither by itself is a criterion for salvation, but it is an indicator of the direction in which you are going.

Although living for Christ is not a matter of following rules, I want to emphasize that belief leads to obedience, two sides of one coin. *What* must be obeyed has been changed throughout history, depending on what God was seeking to accomplish at the time. For instance, Noah was told to build an ark. Did the ark save him, or did his belief—and consequently, his obedience—save him? You might argue one way or the other, but regardless, had he failed to obey, he would not have survived and become key to rebuilding the nations of the earth. God would have found another way. It is the same with Abram. His obedience made it possible for the land of Canaan to become the nation of the Israelites. This principle has been constant throughout the history of God's children. The implication is that only those who *desire* to please God will be *able* to do as they've been asked, and the responsibility is on each individual to find the unique path that God has made for him. He gives us the Spirit to guide us into that knowledge, and He has made all things available to us for our learning, but He will not force obedience. He will not force us to love Him, *for that would not be love.* He will not command our belief, because *that would not be love.* He will not forcibly drag us from our idols that keep us from worshiping Him, because we would continually long for them. It is up to us, so let's find out what this business of choice tells us about God's will, so we can get really busy in making some wonderful choices for Him.

Why do I give this thought so much importance? I do it because it affects how we look at life. If we consider that we are under the drudge of a taskmaster, it affects our attitude. There is a feeling about it that is detrimental to spiritual health. Consequently, we need to change our attitude about obedience from "having to" to "wanting to." "I delight to do your will, O my God, and your law is within my heart" (Psalm 40:8).

Choice

- Who may exercise choice? The right to choose is granted to everyone. As far as we can determine, choice was first given to the angels and was illustrated by Satan's rebellion.
- The angels continued to have choice, as demonstrated by the angelic following that Satan commanded, who were thrown out of heaven along with him after the battle with Michael and his angels (Revelation 12:9). We also know that Adam and Eve were granted choice, as evidenced by Eve's transgression (Genesis 3:6).

- When are you to exercise your choice? (Acts 2:41). Ideally, choice should be exercised as soon as you become the possessor of the knowledge that it is God's will. At that point the responsibility becomes yours; never again will you be able to say, "But Lord, I just didn't know." Another example is of the paralyzed man. He had been bedridden for eight years but was healed and immediately arose to obey Jesus when He said, "Arise and make your bed" (Acts 9:33–34). Can you imagine that man replying, "Oh, just let me rest a few minutes first, Lord. It's been a long eight years"?

- Why did God ordain choice? In my opinion, He authorized choice in order to reveal each person's desire for heaven. It is here that we are allowed to see the brilliance of God's planning. His desire is that every person be reconciled. His knowledge lets Him know that every person would not want salvation, so He lets us choose.

- For what purpose was it utilized? He utilized choice to promote voluntary spiritual growth. He wants to know those who yearn for spiritual enrichment. Remember, He created us in His image, and that image contained the ability to think and to reason. It is possible, therefore, that this purpose may reach into eternity. I believe that the Father will have many things for us to do in eternity, but I doubt that laziness and indolence will be among them. It is very possible that our accomplishments and abilities even the development of the talents we don't feel we truly possess may have some bearing on the things we'll be able to do in eternity. I confess that I am convinced our work here is in some way a preparation for what we will do in our next existence. I'm confident there will be grand surprises when we reach the land of promise. How do things like ignorance affect choice? Ignorance (and probably such things as physical inability to discern) does affect choice. In the case of ignorance, under the old covenant (Mosaic Law), God forgave sins committed in ignorance, "but now commands all men everywhere to repent" (Acts 17:30 NASB). I believe that those who are unable to discern will be treated with the same love and care as infants and small children. "Let the little children come to me, and do not forbid them; for of such is the kingdom of heaven" (Mark 10:14).

I'm hopeful that these questions and answers will help us to understand the difference between a law and a choice. We are so blessed to have forgiveness in the current span of time, but we must recognize that God's sameness—His lack of partiality to any man—means that He also had a plan for the forgiveness of those who lived by faith under the old law and before the law. The plans are the same in that both grant forgiveness by faith in God's promise, but the two promises were a bit different, in that under the old, faith was in a future promise, demonstrated annually by animal sacrifices, while under the new, our faith is in the knowledge that our belief and love for Christ has fulfilled their promise. We also have access to God's throne as often as we wish, which enables our High Priest, Jesus, the Christ to approach Him on our behalf as needed. We have opportunity to claim our changed lives as often as we achieve the goal. Under the old, they had opportunity only once a year. We are so blessed. In this study we *pursue* the righteousness promised as we grow in grace and truth, thus gaining in Spirituality that will help us to serve our Lord and become like Him. Let us therefore renew both our purpose in living and our dedication to the Father as we offer our life for this purpose of love.

4
God's Gentle Care

Love, Respect, Discipline

In the majority of books on building faith, I find that the child is completely left out of the subject. Is this because the writer assumes there is no interest in child rearing unless it is contained within the pages of a book dedicated to the subject? Having raised five daughters, I find this conclusion is erroneous. Children are one of a *parent's* principle motivational purposes for teaching them to grow and live in faith. Your child must not be the dictating center of the family. You, as the adult, should lead your child on a path of discovery. It should be a path that not only teaches him about our Father, but also shows him how to live, by your active pursuit of a life in the Spirit. In this, you will introduce him to the wonder and glory of a relationship with our Father. A child who comes to know the love of the Father through a loving parent learns to love.

A Child's Training

A child's learning capacity is phenomenal and it should be patterned to his level of understanding. Seeking God and learning how to handle choices are not exclusive to adults so it is urgent that we begin the child's training in the home. Ideally, this is where it belongs, because the home is second only in value to the parents. The happier the home is in genuine love and affection, the better prepared the child will be for activities outside of the home.

At birth, a child begins the process of learning and regardless of whether the child is nursed or bottle fed, he must learn how to suckle. Occasionally, this requires great patience for various reasons, and the process can produce tears for both mother and child. Love requires this process of nurturing and ultimately, the outcome is an unbreakable bond of love. This evolves from regular gentle handling, soft talking, fragrance, and warmth, and later the interactions between family and infant. The consistency of these things teaches the infant about how to love and be loved.

Babies grow so fast and learn to make choices every day. As a child gets older and can make the choice to obey Mom or Dad, things get really interesting! The first time he learns that Mom/Dad doesn't mean what is said, the parent is in trouble, and as soon as the parent learns the child has it figured out, they are both in trouble. This annoying situation will be obvious the very first time the parent doesn't follow through with what was instructed, and the child will have learned how to manipulate. The breakdown in teaching is that simple. Speak to your child in love and truth, following Jesus' example with His followers. Speaking without conviction leads to disobedience and rebellion.

Respect and patience are natural outcomes of training a child with an attitude of love. A developing child is very responsive to respect and learns to respect you through the respect he is given. Think about it. You are his live-in example, a huge part of his learning experience. The natural outcome is that he will learn to love and respect others. Watch him as he interacts with playmates and siblings to gauge where he is on this learning continuum. Does he yell at or bully his siblings and playmates, or does he emulate the respect you show him? Be consistent in your teaching and in the consequences for disobedience. There are many methods used to punish disrespect or disobedience, but prevention is the easiest. Your life in prayer and in the Spirit is the key to prevention, because it keeps your aim, your purpose, and your love for the Father and your child at the center of your being.

Since these character traits have their beginning in childhood, it is appropriate to begin the training at the beginning. The importance of purging unwanted character traits before they become lifetime habits should be obvious. It will make for a more contented life for both child and parent and forestall some tougher problems in the future. We are aware from observation (if not actual labor) that the longer that flowers and weeds grow, the sturdier they become and the more difficult they are to prune or (heaven forbid) remove altogether. Roots are either a blessing or a challenge, and so it is with habits.

Sinful habits are not restricted to adults, and it is certainly easier to embed good qualities in children than to do so after they are teenagers or adults. By then, it will be too late or, at the very least, it will not have the benefit of your knowledge and experience. Let me remind you that respect for the child goes a long way in instilling the child's confidence in the teacher (you).

As for a child's spirituality, he will learn this from the actions and the attitudes of those within the home. That is what spirituality is—one's life lived for God. Certainly the "harmful attributes" will be there as well, because we are not perfect examples. God sees you through your heart, so know yourself, and know your heart. It reveals much about the path you are on and hopefully, it is a path that will take you ever closer to our loving Father.

A Warning to Parents

Satan's Ambition

Satan's ambition was to be God (Isaiah 14:13–4). He started a rebellion in heaven and was successful in stealing away a large portion of the heavenly host (Revelation 12:4). Eventually, he declared war on Michael and his angels in heaven but was defeated and thrown out of heaven, "for there was no longer a place for him in heaven" (Revelation 12:7–11). It was then that he turned his attention to man, "who keep the commandments of God and hold to the testimony of Jesus Christ" (Revelation 12:17). This is the war in which we are engaged.

Prior to this defeat in heaven, Satan's war had been primarily a war against God (Hebrews 2:14), but now his attention is focused on man.

Scripture tells us of his defeat (Hebrews 2:14), that he has been judged (John 16:11), and that his sentence of death has been set (Revelation 20:10).

This verse in Hebrews also has some interesting information in regard to Jesus' death and why it was necessary for Him to die after Adam and Eve ate from the Tree of Life. Remember, as we discussed earlier, having eaten of it, they would have lived forever in the depravity of sin because the world as yet had no forgiveness. This would have been pleasing to Satan, who was still in possession of the power over death, but Jesus chose to take the place of animal sacrifice and conquer Satan's power over death by His own death, thus allowing man the choice of eternal life or eternal death. This provided the proof necessary that He is the Son of God—no one but God could resurrect Himself from death. But His death and resurrection also provided for man to have eternal life. You might wonder at this point why the battle continues. As I mentioned in my book, *And There Was War in Heaven*, God's purpose is to save souls; therefore, the war will continue until all things are complete, which means that until God's work is finished (complete) the war will continue. It is *possible*, therefore, that this means that there will be no more souls living who desire salvation.

War with Satan is the nature of the struggle. I know in my mind and in my heart that the moment we think that we have it made, Satan is, at that very moment, creeping about within us to find some damage he can do. I know that my inclination to decline the lead Satan offers is no different from the average person's, except that I know to whom I belong. Don't misunderstand; I don't speak of a supernatural protective shield that surrounds me but of the protection I feel in my heart, and that is from God. There is peace in that knowledge, and it is the same protection the martyrs felt when they refused to deny the crucified Jesus. Possession of that knowledge is the protection that allows anyone, child or adult, to say no at the proper times in life. It carries with it the realization that physical death is not the enemy.

5
Attitudes

Dissension—Division—Destruction

Our religious rivalry resembles that of the Jews as we argue interpretations of Scripture. We are so sure that the interpretation *we* understand is the correct one that we not only refuse to hear differing opinions, but we sometimes even shun those who hold those differing opinions as being less than "authentic" Christians. We would do well to remember Paul's teaching to "gently instruct" in humility, correcting those who are in opposition, while allowing the same privilege of correction to them, leaving to God the responsibility of judging.

I think of an old adage of my mom's and can almost hear her voice: "Now, children, a soft answer turns away wrath." How is it that we seem to have forgotten those old sayings? A little bit of gentleness would work very nicely in our world today; then perhaps God could do the judging and provide the forgiveness, so that both may know the truth. "Holding fast the faithful word as he has been taught, that he may be able, by sound doctrine, both to exhort and convict those who contradict" Titus 1:9. Second Timothy 2:24–25 tells us that when our *attitude* is wrong, some people, who might have been able to understand at a later time, will be completely turned away from Christ. My opinion is that we too often make use of bulldozer tactics instead of "gentle instructing." We forget that we are "seed planters" (Matthew 13:37) and that the harvest is not ours to claim but belongs to God (1 Corinthians 3:6).

To gently instruct bears no resemblance to quarrelling or arguing over God's Word. Another very important factor is that few people are willing to accept another's word about an issue, especially when tempers and voices are raised. We must be ready to discuss these things with interest rather than intimidation. As Paul says, remember to listen and to plant the seed. You don't have to bring your discussion to a conclusion. Leave the door open.

If we question the Israelites' dissension with each other and compare it with our own haughty, egotistical habit of quarreling over opinions, we might want to ask ourselves another question: "How could this lack of love have come about?" There are, of course, many reasons, beginning with the fact that we are human. Aside from that and all of the other reasons that come to mind, I have one to suggest: Satan entered the picture when no one was looking, and love walked out the door. Love simply does not abide where there is dissension and haughtiness. I realize it isn't always easy, but I do believe it can be learned for the sake of teaching, rather than overpowering with rude statements designed to kill with words. This is a time to make use of James 4:6 as a reminder of what you are doing: "God resists the proud, but gives grace to the humble."

Humility needs to be present in all of our dealings with others, regardless of circumstances, and it may be one of the most difficult to achieve, given our own opinions. Jesus humbled Himself to the point of dying on a cross (Philippians 2:8). He did it for the sake of obedience to the Father, but He also did it as an example of how far our obedience must take us, if it is a choice between obeying or forcing our own beliefs on one who is not ready.

As good as our lives are, we should probably never expect that they will be free of problems. Human nature is the warranty on that, and I don't think we need ever be concerned that it will run out. I do not want to leave the false impression that because we are Christians, we should be free of difficulties because of our faith. Struggles to overcome temptation and struggles to survive hard times remain, as do the uncomfortable, painful, annoying distractions that are designed to take us away from God's love. The premise that a follower of Christ will be free of all discomfort and pain is an inaccurate application of a biblical truth. We do know, however, that "the indwelling Spirit is able to overcome sin that previously controlled us" as we grow in strength and devotion. For this reason, He is our leading light who enables the victory over all types of problems that beset us. However, it is possible to over stress this blessing to the extent that we believe that the rougher, tougher side of living for Christ doesn't apply to us. The daily walk in chastening, the endless war with sin and Satan, and the periodic walk in darkness all remain. God did not create His plan to make us weak and unable. He created it to make us strong. The Spirit is our means of making the correct choices to struggle through without losing faith.

If you say to yourself, "I believe," that is great, but the demons also "believe and tremble" (James 2:19). This is because they cannot (or will not) bring themselves to obey. I give this quotation to demonstrate that belief is not the end; it is the beginning. God has more truths for us than we can ever get around to, so we must stay alert, rejoice in our relationship with Him, and seek out, with curiosity, those things He allows us to know for our edification. I found a great quote in the book *Life in the Spirit* by A. W. Tozer, in which he comments, "Belief buried under inactivity and the lack of attention is of no use to anyone."[14] I agree with this assessment.

Mr. Tozer reminds us that an inactive truth is worthless. He is speaking of God's truths. An example: if you know to care for those in need and do nothing that 'truth' is *worthless in your life* as Mr. Tozer says. However, it *does not invalidate the truth itself.* Unfortunately, recognition of error in an abstract situation is more difficult to identify. My point is that as we study God's Word, we need to keep an open mind to the explanation that the Spirit is trying to give. Preconceived ideas mislead. If you don't immediately understand what you are reading, set it aside, and come back to it fresh, after prayer and meditation. Use caution in asking others for their interpretations, because this is one of Satan's tools for dissension. It is the old principle that says, "Divide and conquer." Another point to consider is that you don't *have* to be on the same page as anyone else in your understanding. What counts in your life is the conclusion *you* have drawn from your own study, hence the need to be active in studying God's Word. Each of us is on an individual timeline. Change, in the sense of growth,

---

[14] A. W. Tozer, *Life in the Spirit,* copyright 2009 by Hendrickson Publishers Marketing, LTC, in agreement with Wingspread Publishers, titled Filled With the Holy Spirit, 2nd edition December 2011.

may put someone way behind where you are or light-years ahead. Actually, differences are great and make for interesting discussions. If only we could see it that way and not feel that there is only one way of looking at things, especially when it's a discussion that's spiritual. Well, at least it should be spiritual. If we are able to listen, we can say, you may be right. Why don't we pray about this a bit more and maybe get in a little more research and we may agree on this yet. If we don't, that's not a problem either, we just both need to keep searching and we'll get back together later. Is that a deal? And then as you leave, say something like, Hey, I want you to know that I really appreciate your thoughts on this.

Let me give you a statement of my own conviction: differences are healthy. Let me explain. I believe they are healthy because they make us think. Thinking is good, especially as we continue to search the Scriptures daily. Much more dangerous to our faith is the attitude that says, "You do things my way or else." And before you know it, Christians are again divided by misunderstandings and hot tempers. Insisting on one interpretation is an insidious threat and very deadly to Christianity. In fact, it has "division" splashed all over it. Take a look at the Corinthian Church. Not only were their ideas at odds, but in some cases they had crossed the boundary line of consensus and were downright sinful. Still, Paul addressed them as "brethren" and counseled them in love as he reproved those who were practicing immorality. Then he taught again on issues that were divisive, in the hope of achieving better understanding. The virtues taught by Peter would have said, "Continue to study, and if you persevere, in time, godliness and brotherly kindness will provide the necessary love to resolve this issue."

It is sad to realize how quickly Christians began to argue. It is not only sad, but it also demonstrates a lack of understanding of God's principles. With the death, resurrection, and ascension of Jesus and the beginning of the church, God's beloved people had a new beginning with His Son the head. His plan had proved to be successful. His promise to Abraham fulfilled. His people were able to move from the bondage of the Law to the freedom in Christ, but it was a choice, not a demand. The gift was offered. Acceptance was now left to the individual. Now is the best time ever to say, "Lord, I believe; help my unbelief" (Mark 9:24).

We are discussing dissension because God presents us with choice, which by its definition and nature implies differences. The "I'm right and you're wrong" attitude is deadly, not only in regard to opinions but also methods. The process of learning is different for each of us, at least to some extent, and is not to be condemned. Remember, it was the law that said, "Do it or be condemned," yet God's grace provided access to Christ's blood and forgiveness even then. We need to practice the grace of God in our relationships with those who hold different ideas, and it wouldn't hurt to add a little diplomacy as well. Remember as you struggle with these issues that the Christian's responsibility for judging is limited to the one in the church who practices immorality. *All other judging belongs to God.*

Remember Pentecost and the joy that pervaded the city and that brought a great number of people together in the harmony of fellowship. People were excited, and excitement is contagious. It drew people who asked questions, giving opportunity for the new Christians to tell the story of Jesus. It was then that the Spirit was able to touch hearers with understanding. Are we telling that story, or have we forgotten that it is the gospel that pricks men's hearts? Without the believing heart, even the Spirit cannot do the job He is meant to do. One of the points of this discussion is that the birthright of every Christian is joy, but the only way joy can become a blessing in our lives is if we are able also to use other godly principles to resolve differences. Even if differences are not resolved, love must remain.

Debates, Beneficial or Harmful

For many years, speakers (usually ministers) came together in a public forum for what was called debates. People of all faiths came to hear the discussions, held in high-volume rhetoric, and for a number of years, it was considered great entertainment, and it continued for weeks as those in the attendance argued with each other about who had won the debate. I know that this practice was prevalent in the eastern states and that it welcomed some of the great orators from England and Scotland (and perhaps other countries of which I am unaware). There was also a wagon train of Christians who migrated to Oregon, carrying this practice into the northwestern part of the United States. As the population moved westward, it wasn't long before the practice had completely spread from east to west. In retrospect, the "debate" fever seemed like a truck with no brakes – unstoppable. Believers would assemble two or three times a week to hear these men argue their doctrinal issues that could have been attributed to a dueling match except that their "guns" were words and winning was the name of the game. I called it death and destruction by words.

The debates were not all bad. In addition to providing entertainment, there were some good points on both sides, but I have often wondered if anyone ever was convinced by the opposing side. When I say some of it was good, I'm referring to the result of intense study on both sides of whatever issue was up for discussion. Even so, the argumentative tone was a black spot on Christ's entire message. It set the stage for the quarrelsome nature of the religious community that has existed ever since. In a few instances, hate brought the end result of death in the north east and it is more than fair to say, our Lord was not glorified. Murder, as God tells us in Matthew 5:21–24, is the end result of anger and hate. Of course there are instances of infamy throughout the Bible, because we are all human, with characteristics that are often more like Satan's than the ones God would like us to have. Communities of believers usually follow their leaders, and hateful in-fighting takes its toll to some degree still today.

The danger of this type of "teaching," if you can call it teaching is that the whole thing is contrary to God's will for us. He desires unity and peace between believers. Does that mean we must have opinions that are carbon copies? No, in fact even the suggestion that God wants us to be robotic herd followers is in error. We have great need to follow God's non-negotiable rules and to grow in spiritual virtues, but not by bringing animosity to our understanding of the principles that guide us.

C. S. Lewis called the use of self-promoting arguments "a ghastly simplicity which removes results yet demands moral function."[15] He said that we fail to consider the results that come from such undisciplined emotional confrontations but nonetheless demand to look on them as useful. His conclusion is that we are able to practice self-control "only

---

[15] Norman L. Geisler, *Baker Encyclopedia of Christian Apologetics* (Grand Rapids, MI: Baker Academic, 2005), 42.

because we stand within God's law" and are powerless to do so without trained emotions.[16]

Mr. Lewis goes on to say, "There must be an objective, universal moral law, or else no ethical judgments make sense. Furthermore, we are bound by that law, though it did not originate with us, and therefore, there exists a Moral law-giver who is the ultimate source and standard of all right and wrong."[17]

I draw the conclusion that unless we allow the Spirit access to our hearts and minds through the loving teaching of values, morals, and ideals, we will slip from the precarious pinnacle upon which we have come to rest (which might be interpreted as the first principles of Christ) and will slowly or precipitously return to our starting place. Again, God provides the right of choice. We can say, "No, thank you," to spiritual teaching. We can say yes, but manage to continually quench the Spirit. Or we can say yes and develop our ability to hear and to see His results in others, as well as to feel them within our own lives. The choice is ours. *Do we have the appropriate desire to accommodate the spiritual growth we need?* A decision is a good starting place, but alone, it is weak. It must be shored up by spiritual concepts, such as prayer, self-discipline, and praise for the Father as we worship Him daily in the lives we present to the world.

As we communicate we are inclined to assume that we are understood as intended. This is seldom the case. How often have you heard someone say when quoted, "But that's not what I was saying!"? It is unlikely that any person is going to understand exactly as *we* understand what we say. It is not only the manner in which we express our ideas (our speech) but also the manner in which we listen. We need to extend courtesy to others because we are Christians, even if there is no other reason to do so, and while we are doing that, we also need to cut some slack with regard to what we *think* we hear, and remember to listen more and talk less. Hearing is an art that involves real listening that hears with the heart.

Another reason others are unlikely to agree with expressed opinions (regardless of which side we are on) is that arguers are generally arbitrary. It would be well to remember that God says of this situation that He may grant repentance to the hearer, assuming he was in error (2 Timothy

---

16 Geisler *Baker Encyclopedia of Christian Apologetics*, 42.

17 Geisler, *Baker Encyclopedia of Christian Apologetics*, 42.

2:25). Why would God grant repentance? He grants repentance because it precedes forgiveness and is of itself a request for forgiveness. The conclusion is that attitude matters and the attitude needed is one of love. So if you do not drive someone away with an ungodly attitude, it is possible that repentance will come at a later time, and God will both forgive and open the heart of the one who couldn't understand.

When I was a child, an old gospel preacher impressed me with these words of advice: "Always leave the door open for another person to build on what you have started." Good advice.

6

Tools for Guidance

Developing the Spirit

Tools are the jewels that enable any serious occupation. Without them we are lost. For instance if a writer chooses to write on a particular subject but is unable to choose an emphasis, he can go to almost an endless variety of places such as the internet, books, people to find just the right angle. When it comes to tools however, I offer nothing new. These well-used, sometimes neglected tools are ageless. Practical and easy to use, they fit in the manner of a smooth glove or an old shoe. Slip them on as you wake each morning, and you'll rest better as daylight fades and peaceful sleep beckons.

Prayer

Demonstrating change requires an overhaul of priorities, followed by giving self to the Holy Spirit as a vessel to be filled with His blessings for our spiritual growth. To my mind, the most logical first step in seeking this guidance is to pattern ourselves after our Savior; specifically, in accordance with His prayer life. Seriously! Even though my first thought was, "Of course He didn't *need* to pray as we do." Ever thought that? You are absolutely *right*! Why did He do it, then, so regularly? He did it because *He wanted to talk with the Father.* There you have it, and *that* is our very first problem. We look on it as something we have to do instead of something we want to do, and immediately our resistance kicks in. Jesus looked on it as a blessing, one that He couldn't get through a day without. So in using this as an example, the first thing I want us to know is that Jesus' prayer life is a wonderful example, but even more fundamentally, it was a part of His life.

Jesus prayed constantly. He prayed alone; at times, He prayed all night. He prayed publicly. He prayed in times of crisis, and He prayed before events. He prayed for others, and He prayed for Himself. He prayed for sinners, and He prayed for saints (that's us—His followers). His prayers included thanksgiving and praise for the Father. His prayers were always in submission to the Father (Luke 22:42), and they were offered in an attitude of love and humility (Matthew 6:6). *Prayer is our number-one method for spiritual growth.* I have used this method of comparison to help us see that first, we must figure out how to change our attitude about prayer. How are we to move from the position of "have to" to "want to," while remembering that prayer must be a constant in the life we live for Him? We must *start*! Beginning is the first clue. Do you want this change of attitude? If you *do*, get on your knees and tell Him that you do, asking for forgiveness and strength as you praise him for who He is. Attitudes only change with doing. In time, self-serving will become God-fearing obedience, and His grace will welcome you with open arms. Humility is the next step up!

Humility

As we come to the Father in humility, we learn that the act itself is a blessing. How is it that we are able to talk with God the Father? We understand that our words must come from the heart. We must tell Him that we worship and praise Him because He is God. We must thank Him for the beauty of the creation in which He chose to surround us; for life and blessings; for the lives of our loved ones. We must praise Him for all that He is and all that He does for man, and we must acknowledge our unworthiness. We must thank Him for the gift of His Son, for forgiveness, and for reconciliation and the hope of life eternal with Him.

We do not need grand words or big words, but we do need heartfelt words, spoken in deep love, that Jesus took our place on that cross so long ago. Let your heart agonize over that sacrifice, silently knowing that He hears the unspoken words of your heart. Then talk to Him about the pain you feel and how it fills you with grief that can only be assuaged by His love. You will come to realize that the more you talk to Him of this, the more real it becomes to you, and the more you will begin to feel Him in your heart, your soul, and your mind, and the better you will want to know Him. You'll find you'll make fewer requests of Him, although He wants you to tell Him of your needs. Perhaps you'll tell Him more of your spiritual needs and less of your physical needs, and He will be pleased with your growth. You'll say thank you more often that He blesses you in His omniscience, rather than by those requests you made that sometimes now seem foolish. Then you can tell Him in all honesty, "Lord, my only need is for you," and suddenly you will know why Jesus prayed all the time. You'll know that you have acquired the same need through His example, because it is a matter of devotion.

Submission

We have just seen that humility must be a part of our prayer life. This next quotation illustrates that humility is also a part of submission: "Submitting to one another in the fear of God" (Ephesians 5:21). "Let nothing be done through selfish ambition or conceit, but in lowliness of mind let each esteem others better than himself" (Philippians 2:3). Wow! That really sets it up for us. Submission is a method of growth that requires humility. These two qualities are not overly admired in our nation or in our society. I am afraid they have been largely neglected, if not totally ignored in our lives.

Wisdom dictates the use of appreciation rather than accusation, of respect rather than disdain. Each example takes us back to love as one of the non-negotiable laws that goes all the way back to Mount Sinai and the giving of the old covenant. As I've mentioned, this is basic to a follower of Christ, and it is interesting that it applies not only to specific categories of people but to all people and all relationships.

This places living for Christ in humility and submission as a by-product of living in love. At least we need to know and practice humility as an ingredient in loving others. Have you ever considered if you are submissive to others? Submission to one another definitely requires humility. Humility is a method of growth. It is an attitude but one that must come from the heart. Fake humility is insulting and damages relationships. What does humility mean to us as followers of Christ? It means we have a responsibility to treat all people with respect in love, regardless of race, color, or economic level. What does that mean? I think it means that we treat others in the same way we would like them to treat us. It should also indicate that I, as a child of God, recognize that I don't know it all. How hard is it to say at the end of a discussion, "You may be correct, let me think and pray about this and perhaps we can talk again"?

As humility settles about you, you'll find that you are able to grasp a greater and perhaps deeper sense of the submission that guided our Lord. Arrogance is not possible where humility exists. The Son of God possessed the fullness of God, even while He walked the earth as a human being. "For in Him all the fullness of Deity dwells in bodily form" (Colossians 1:19). If ever one could have been arrogant, it would have been our Lord, but He was not. In fact, He was submissive to the point of death (Philippians 2:8). What does that say to us individually? It tells me that our Lord's submission was an act of willing martyrdom and that ours *can be*, by the same reason of commitment and dedication. When we make the choice to follow Him, it is an internal martyrdom that says, "Your will be done." We must do away with ungodly attitudes.

Study

If we want to please Him, we must learn to study—and dare I say, enjoy it? It is an art form. Don't do the same things over and over, unless it is beneficial to you. How can you know what God requires of you without study? If you are living on the fumes of some studying you did a long time ago, you may be reaching the point of desperation for spiritual nourishment. This tool is invaluable and connects in the same ways that prayer and humility do. Don't ever skimp on prayer and study. It is common knowledge that claiming a specific time for these activities, combined with an additional amount of time for meditation, is the best way to be certain you will obtain your time with God.

The act of study prevents us from being taken in and confused by crafty and deceitful doctrine, while truth in love allows growth and edification (Ephesians 4:14–16), it is only through this method that the body of Christ can work together, with each doing a share for the edification of all in order that all may be edified. Devotion is an outcome of such discipline, along with dedication and co-operation, while each is a tool that serves in the transformation to spirituality (Ephesians 4:14–16).

If you wonder how to obey an abstract perception, let me explain it this way: It is true that belief and faith are both abstract perceptions, but nothing at all is abstract about obedience. Like the apostle James told us, obedience is the proof of one's faith, and it is the proof that provides transformation to both participants in this transaction. That is spirituality.

Let's look at an example of how studying can become viable. If you continually do the same thing day after day, it is going to get stagnant. "In Him was life, and the life was the light of men" (John 1:4). In a literal sense, we could say that "in Him was life" says He was alive, but we're fortunate because we know it says more. If we look at the second part of the sentence and try to figure out how John means this to be a truth to live by, then we need to know *how* it can be accomplished. First, we need to identify the person John refers to as "Him," and He is identified as Jesus who is more than alive; He is God's Son, and though He lived on earth as a human, "in Him is all the fullness of the Father."

The rest of John's sentence finishes the thought, "and the life was the light of men." Do we understand this to be an ordinary light or a different kind of light?

The light of which John spoke was no ordinary light, for there is something that sets it apart: "and the light was the light of men." What does that say, and what does it mean? What do lights do in regular language?

1. They get rid of darkness. (If you don't understand you're in the dark, what can you know?)
    *   Answer: Research the information; don't make decisions in the darkness of little or no knowledge

2. They enable one to see! (If you can't see clearly, you don't know what you have and can easily be misled.)
   - Answer: Seeing is vital to understanding.

3. They identify things.
   - Answer: It has been suggested that personal experience and study are great identifiers that could be compared to touching, feeling, listening, holding, and meditation.

To show you how reading the book of John has changed for me, when I first began to study it, I thought there wasn't much to it, because it seemed so simple. Now I know better; I was so wrong. Look again, and you will find yourself blessed.

These tools are such great "people tools"; try it sometime for the satisfaction of settling differences of opinion as they encroach upon your life. Such things as prayer, humility, and submission, combined with study and an active faith, smooth any path you're on. Know why? Nobody—I mean, *nobody*—can fake those five tools. Not when they are all together and at the *same time*. Know what I mean? Let's say them again: prayer, humility, submission and study, combined with an active faith. These five tools will enable you to experience the joy of your birthright in Christ Jesus. They will also develop a momentum in your desire to know Him, and you will experience an upsurge of devotion as you worship Him in prayer. This is spiritual growth.

As spiritual attitudes become more a part of your daily life, you may realize that you are feeling ready for a "one size fits all" sweep of conscience to rid it of the ghosts of selfishness, greed, inflated ego, jealousy, envy, hate, cruelty, and a failure to love that were a part of your life in the past. This is a special moment. You may want to get down on your knees in gratitude to the Spirit who has guided you in this path. As you express your gratitude, you suddenly remember Jesus' praying on the cross for those who have placed him there, and as realization overwhelms your conscience, you may want to pray for them as well. For you have suddenly realized that your own rebellious acts also placed Him on that awful tree, and you cry out "Father, we didn't know" (Luke 23:34)!

As you think about this you are also able to recognize that your forgiveness and your knowledge of things spiritual would not be, without that shedding of blood and again you whisper, "Forgive us Father, bless our recognition of that fact that your Son may be glorified as others come to obedience). With deep gratitude and renewed devotion I acknowledge that I was the one who should have died. Father, for the Entirety of your great and wondrous gift I thank you. Amen."

This new feeling, which you may recognize as momentum, will come from the dedication of purpose to continue in the progress you are making in your quest for spiritual growth. When you begin to feel energetic and ready to be busy for the Lord, you will most likely have an urge to find something to do immediately. *Wait.* Continue to pray and think of the Scripture, "Be still and know that I am God" (Psalm 46:10). When He sees that you are ready, He will reveal His plan for you. You may not recognize what is happening. Remember the apostle John on Patmos, who prepared himself by "being in the Spirit" (Revelation 1:10). This refers to an attitude of worship. Consider carefully your role in fulfilling His will, because while God's plan is infallible, your own part is not. Pray before, during, and after as you carry out His will, because what you do *must represent Him in praise and glory.* You do not want it to bring shame on Him, on the church, or on yourself, so you must act in wisdom, with the knowledge that you are serving God, not yourself.

7

A Child's Introduction to God

A Childs Spiritual Journey

When I was very young and cried for attention, my granny would hold me as she rocked and crooned, "It's okay, baby. Granny loves you if no one else does," which referred to the fact that everyone in the house was busy doing something vital. Then my granny died, and for days I wandered aimlessly, in ignorance of what had happened. Finally, a guest in the house lifted me up so that I could see inside a "funny bed" that sat in the middle of the room. I was very surprised to see my granny asleep there, and I wondered why she was sleeping in the living room. I did grasp that she wouldn't be sleeping with me anymore, and that made me sad. The same year, my oldest sister, at age fifteen, left home for college at Oklahoma A&M. I don't remember her at all from that time, but I heard the conversations about her, and I would ask, "Who are you talking about?" The answer was always, "Your sister," so I knew someone was gone who had been with us, and that reminded me of Granny. I would ask, "Is she in heaven with God?" and since the answer was no, I had something new to think about.

Four years later, school began for me in Delhi, Oklahoma, where we had lived for some time. I was excited about school, because it meant I would learn how to read. I was, I think, an imaginative child who pretended to write before I could spell. I would copy letters carefully, eager then to know what they said. Still very stubborn about this subject of reading and writing, I learned to read the first day of school by disobeying my teacher's instructions to look or read the few pages we were "given permission" to see. I was punished with a scowl of disapproval, not to mention the shame of carrying home a note to inform my parents of my transgression. This is the same me who, that same year, was scared to death of participating in an Easter egg roll in a grassy field. Sure enough, as soon as I moved from my safe spot, someone plowed into me, and I lost all of the eggs I'd been given. You can see from this experience that I really wanted to read that book. Desire was what gave me courage. Where there is no desire, there's no courage.

After that year of school, we returned to Texas, and after living in Lubbock and then Denver City, one school year each, we moved to Abilene. I fell in love immediately with Abilene because of the beautiful trees, which turned out to be mesquites and were not thought of very highly. No matter; I loved them and still think they're beautiful and full of character and charm. From Lubbock I was promoted from second to fourth grade. I didn't look at my report card that summer, nor did my parents, so when school started in the fall, I went into third grade and found a seat. The class was about to begin, when a lady came in to get me, saying, "Come with me, honey. You're in the fourth grade." Well! For a good while I felt cheated out of third grade, but I got over it. I was eight.

We went next to Abilene, where Mother found a church not too far away. Not having a car or knowing anyone in the city, we all got ready and walked to church. The "not too far" turned out to be more than a mile, one way, and we made it to church twice on Sundays; we were allowed to miss on Wednesday evenings as the weather cooled. There was a railroad track right in the center of the length of that walk and a major highway in and out of Abilene on the south side of the tracks. I was very impressed with this new arrangement and so were my parents. We felt at home somehow, and we came to know and love the people and the trees, so we decided to stay. Fortunately, God agreed, and Daddy found work to support our already diminished family. If you remember, Granny had died several years before, and Aunt Pary (better known as Parthena Clementine) had gone back to her twin sister, Aunt Melly (Melsinna Haseltine).

In this new place, God helped us a lot. Outside of regular day-to-day living, He did some long-range planning, and before we left Abilene, He had found husbands for sisters numbers two and three. Sister number one had left the educational field and was flagging down cargo planes in New York City (this was during WWII). My brother and I were all that was left, and I reckoned we'd better start initiating our own plans for the future before God found someone for us to marry too! I was not ready to follow in the sisters' footsteps. Before I had a chance to talk to my brother about this feeling, he was gone. He'd joined the army, and I was without all my siblings. Life was very difficult.

We made lots of friends in the new congregation, or at least Mother and Daddy did, and then one day, a lovely, slim, dark-haired girl came to me, and we talked, and I went home with her for dinner. Suddenly, I knew I had a friend.

By the end of that year, I decided I had waited long enough to be baptized.

How much did I know at nine? Not much. I knew quite a number of Bible stories, but how they correlated to God's will that I be baptized, I had no inkling. But here are some things that filled my mind at the time, things I felt I knew, but other things I was concerned about:

- I knew that God loved me and had given His life for me so that I could have forgiveness for all my sins.
  (Paradoxically, I wondered what my sins were).
- I knew that God was preparing a place for me to live with Him when I died, and I really wanted to be there.
- I knew in my heart that God wanted me to do something for Him, but I had no idea what it was.
- I also knew that He wanted me to follow Him, to be a Christian, although I didn't know the distinction between the Father and the Son, with no ideas at all about the Holy Spirit and not too much understanding of what "Christian" meant; the words 'to follow' puzzled me because God was invisible.

I worried about it for some time and wondered if I would be allowed this decision. Finally, on a Sunday evening, I took my courage in hand

and, shaking like a leaf, I scooted out into what seemed a very long aisle and headed for the front of row after row of benches filled with people who were all looking at me. All went well, and I was baptized that night by the minister of the congregation, who was by then a friend of my family. It felt good. It felt right, and I was happier than I could ever remember feeling. In addition, I experienced a peaceful feeling I'd not felt since my granny had died. Deep down inside me, I also had a feeling of being responsible for something but still didn't know what it was. Also, I recognized the feeling of belonging. I loved my family, but I also knew I belonged to God now.

I wish I could say I never lost the calm or the joy that came with the aftermath of my baptism, but my story isn't a miracle; it is just a child's view of God's will and a child's heart that knew it wanted to belong to Him. Even though I was unable to retain the joy and the peace I had experienced earlier, I did keep the feeling of belonging and the sense of responsibility.

This was my introduction to God. Though my recollection of the events and the feelings that led up to it are incomplete, I'm happy to have shared this experience with you.

A Child's Sin

It is only fair now that you hear a little about the time during which I was the most rebellious. By no means would you call me a perfect child. It is far more normal to say I did not change much until many years later, when the lessons began to soak into my stubborn head. In the three incidents I revealed to you from my early childhood, I had no doubt at all about doing what I alone decided to do. In retrospect, it is interesting to me that of the three, I made one right decision—following God—and two that were not in my best interest. Obedience was non-negotiable in my family, but I learned that desire can overpower that teaching. In the long run, it was a valuable lesson to learn.

I saw my baptism as being between God and me, and it didn't seem I should have to consult with anyone, but going beyond what I was told

I could do was a deliberate act of rebellion, even though I was only six. I see it as a tentative probe by Satan into my soul, and, as with Eve, he achieved his purpose and found a weak spot within me. I share this as an example that such a small thing can still be wrong, because it is an act of stubborn will.

I'm going to share a couple of incidents now from a different period of my life, not because these happenings are dramatically different but because in some ways (if you think of principles rather than the similarities of the events), they are very much alike.

It seemed that adults now considered me mature enough to be honest, worthy of trust, and responsible. Read and see what you think. Although the timing is different than the previous references, I still was quite young, and the transgressions (see how we avoid the word sin?) were a bit more complicated, but I still was thinking about me.

The first memory I'll share involves going to the little neighborhood store for my mother on my bike for some cooking necessity. I was given the exact amount of change for the purchase, including tax. I was thrilled to be allowed to go this far on my bike and set off proudly confident that I was a big girl now. Mother inadvertently sent too much money, and temptation set in. As explanation, even though it isn't an excuse, I must add that as children, we never had pennies, much less nickels or dimes, to spend as we liked, and by some magic, there was exactly the amount I needed for a particular candy I desired—a Val-o-Milk. This delicacy had a gooey white vanilla center wrapped in luscious milk chocolate, and there were two muffin-like pieces in each package. I don't recall that I even hesitated. I put the money down and made a very slow business of getting to my bike. (I had to eat the whole thing before I could arrive home.) I had already violated mother's trust; now I made her wait while I ate the delicious forbidden fruit. Then I lied to her. Unknown to me at the time, the storekeeper had put the cash register tape in my grocery bag. Mother didn't tell me how she knew what I'd done, but by that time in my life, I was convinced she could see out of the back of her head anyway, as she always knew what we — brother and sisters — were up to. It was an episode I shall remember with clarity, even after I have breathed my last. Even worse than the paddling she gave me was my knowledge of how much I had disappointed her.

The other incident involved a note from my teacher, requesting that I be allowed to go with another girl to town on a Saturday to purchase a prize gift for a contest that was conducted in our classroom. Unknown to my teacher and my mother, the other girl was babysitting several brothers and sisters, and they were all going with us, because their mother had told them they could see a movie afterward. I asked my mother if I could stay for the movie, but she told me to come straight home afterward; I still had my chores to do when I got home. In the several blocks of walking to town, temptation began. "No one will know," they said. And they had enough money to buy my ticket. I was easily convinced, because the movie starred Sonia Henie, an Olympic ice-skating star. I had drooled with longing for days over the advertisement in the local paper, wishing there was some way I could see this sparkling movie. Obviously, I hadn't learned my lesson over the Val-o-Milk well enough, and since I was older now, the consequences were more severe. I remember being grounded for a *long* time, getting more chores to do, and having my bike taken away. What is most revealing is that I was still fighting the battle of the Val-o-Milk. Would this battle ever end?

In the first episode, what started out as joy ended in shame and punishment. I broke trust. I lied and cheated, all for a 'treat' I took from my mother without permission. Isn't that stealing? "But you were only a child," you may say. You are correct, but I was a very well-taught child who had made promises to God, and I had broken them, and then I lied to my mother.

In the second incident, I recall not wanting to go on that little shopping trip because this classmate was not very pretty (shame on me), and she dressed funny (where was my compassion?), and she had a posse of raucous children with her (it was obvious that taking care of these children was a regular responsibility for her). Satan took care of all of my hesitations by giving me what I wanted more than anything I could imagine ever wanting in this world—the Sonja Henie movie. To begin with, I was trusted to do an errand in an adult manner, but I didn't want the responsibility. I had a very bad attitude about this classmate, who was a very nice, tired, obedient girl who was willing to give up some of her nickels and dimes so I could share a movie with her and fulfill my selfish desire.

Can you see how such a seemingly innocent sin can seem up front, yet be so very deadly in a spiritual sense? It's no different, really, from what we are likely to do as adults, except for the age of the one who does it. My point is that sin doesn't wait. Satan catches followers at even younger ages. Though I hated the punishments I received for such wrongdoing, I truly am thankful for it as an adult. It has made me stronger, believe me. How? Oh, in the most important way possible. I can look right in Satan's eyes now and say 'get lost, no one here even wants you around; beat it. You're a rotten, conceited, selfish trouble-maker.' And when he runs from me – (understand what I'm saying?) – when he runs from me – it is a sight to remember: James 4:7 "Resist the devil and he will run from you"!

What is even more important to my learning process I was finally able to connect the wrong I did to what I had done and I was thinking selfishly, thinking of what 'I' wanted. This little story illustrates the fact that Satan attacks the mind which is the thinking tool of the body. Being tempted as I've said before is not a sin. The candy was the tool Satan used to encourage my selfishness and because it worked he used it again with the incident of the movie. I hated that knowledge more than I had hated the punishment received. So the next thing I did was to shift the blame from 'me' to my Mother. I was not angry with God but with my mother, blaming her for being strict. Yeah, right. Have you ever heard that before? Kids are slippery sometimes. Without even thinking, they'll let you take the blame for them. Listen to what they have to say, and be fair, but don't be the victim for them. That could set a pattern that could be very damaging to you both. I remained angry with Mother for a while but eventually, I knew that she had punished me out of love, in the same manner God punishes the people of the world when we rebel, so that He can teach us, through His love, a better way to live. If you are feeling punished, I suggest you become familiar with Proverbs 3:11-2 "...do not reject the discipline of the Lord or loathe His reproof, for whom the Lord loves He reproves" (NASB).

The Application

In retrospect, I am able to give my *need* for God a little more definition. There are probably reasons that I was motivated to seek the comfort of God at such an early age, but the only clue I have is my relationships with family. I have come to believe that this early alignment with God *created a bond* that is not as easily broken, perhaps, as one where life has set different agendas that are sometimes contrary to God's will. By learning His will at an early stage in my life, I have experienced a confidence in Him that has very often made decisions easier. At the same time, it has helped to heal much of my lack of self-confidence. Many come to the Lord at later times in life, and the blessings they experience are equally beneficial and should be shared with those who are not yet believers but seekers.

One of the blessings I feel I gained is the knowledge of His surrounding presence. I often call it a hovering presence, and He is there whether I work or play. He is also a presence *within me*, and I can finally recognize Him as the Spirit. He is my strength, my rock. The fact that I have always seen Him as God the Father undoubtedly goes back to my early knowledge of God, the Father alone. As I mentioned earlier, I had no concept at the time of the Trinity. I believe They are all willing to understand that discrepancy, for they are one. I also believe that I got the word "hovering" from Genesis 1:2, which is a description of the Spirit but which, at the time, meant God to me, which meant the Father.

Will I ever be free of the burden of selfishness? This is a good question because it can refer to any of the – "selfisms" of which we seek to rid ourselves. As a matter of conscious thinking, I believe that we can be free of these specific burdens with the help of the Spirit. Satan does, however, know the way into your heart, so be consistent in your will to be free of his influence.

Personally – at the time – I found it strange that I hadn't learned much. I realized almost immediately upon analysis that I had been interested only in what *I wanted*. Don't you find it extremely discouraging to learn what a 'twerp' you are? Like most people (probably) I wanted to be thought of in a complimentary way. I have no idea if my determination to improve who I wanted to be began at that moment or if it waited another two or three years before any changes kicked in. What I *do* know is that something about my attitude clicked into tune with what was happening and I saw just a tiny bit of hope for me. Would it be the beginning of a metamorphosis? Probably in lieu of my 'then' vocabulary I wouldn't have called it metamorphosis, but something very dull, like improvement 'maybe'.

8

Motivation

The Will to Be

"The characteristic of a disciple is not that he does good things, but that he is good in his motives, having been made good by the supernatural grace of God. The only thing that exceeds right-doing is right-being."[18] (Note: this particular publication by Mr. Chambers has no page numbers, but each page is marked with a date.)

In a nutshell, Oswald Chambers is telling us that right motives give us the ability to be better than we are. He quotes Matthew 5:20. "Except your righteousness exceeds the righteousness of the scribes and Pharisees, you will by no means enter the kingdom of heaven." What exactly did the scribes and Pharisees consider right-doing? The Pharisees focused on external obedience only, meaning to the letter of the law, with all i's dotted and t's crossed, very legalistic. No aspect of the law could be left undone evidently even the clerical accuracy. However, this approach was without any consideration of the internal conformity to the spirit of the law that Jesus taught.

Chambers points out that the Pharisees thought they followed the law, but were not doing so, because they left faith out of it. As they went through the motions of 'what' to do, they were 'obeying' only because they

---

[18] Oswald Chambers Assoc. Ltd., *My Utmost for His Highest Journal* (Uhrichsville, Ohio: Barbour Publishing, Inc., 1992), 7/24.

felt they *had* to. God wanted their obedience because they loved Him, *not* because He said it is my will. This is still the way God sees it, so we must keep it in the forefront of our minds as we consider motivation.

The next thing we need to understand is that God expects our work to be motivated by love. To deviate from such motivation could be the worst crime (sin) against Him we are capable of committing. Think about it and keep it in your consciousness. It is possibly worse than doing nothing because gifts that pretend to love are demeaning. They say to the recipient, "I don't really even like you, but I'm doing my duty and I sure hope you get your act together soon." We probably would never actually say such a thing, but it is difficult to hide the attitude. Think of Jesus and His love, beginning with the gift of Himself. Try, then, to be a little (or a lot) more loving on a day by day schedule and make a chart to record your progress and your failures. As you do these things remember the servant who hid his one talent and was consequently thrown into darkness when the Master returned because he hadn't tried to earn any profit for his master. Not trying with God is failure.

The Pharisees (or we) could do everything perfectly and Jesus would still be unhappy if what was done was not out of love. On the other hand Chamber's example is a perfect illustration. *Spirit-induced nature* (love), which is of God, makes one greater than by doing the right thing and is known as the spiritual characteristic *right-being*, of which Chambers speaks. Since one of my favorite expressions is that we need to "be" for Him, I really like this comparison. Do you think we, in this day and age, are in any way caught up in "having to do," or do we "do" out of love for the purity that God demands, that comes from within? It is a question we each should ask and answer for self.

This is a demonstration of the walk with God. You either fit into that category as you live by God's principles, or you hedge with excuses and don't. Another really interesting fact, however, is that many in the world fit the pattern of Cornelius, who was a devout man who prayed daily to God but who didn't know Him. Such a person's good works would not be credited to God. James' letter to the scattered Christians addresses this situation by teaching that such benevolence does not need to be halted, but rather the giver must be taught proper motivation (James 2:19). This is the situation with Cornelius, a just, God-fearing Roman centurion.

Peter is brought into the situation by direct intervention of God, and in Acts, we learn the result of what was taught through the messenger, Peter. Cornelius, his kinsmen, and his friends upon hearing the Word of God and witnessing the power of the Holy Spirit and hearing those who spoke in tongues magnify God, realized that God is not a respecter of persons, and were therefore baptized as Peter commanded them. Those who came with Peter were witness to the happening, as these were the first Gentiles to receive the Word of God. This is a good place to repeat that no one can become pure by obeying rules and regulations. The teachings of Christ are *truths* that can only be interpreted by His nature which is placed within us through the Holy Spirit. *This* is why we must learn as much as possible about His nature in order to better form our own into His image.

I hope you noticed that the coming of the Spirit and the joyful reaction of the Romans and all who were with Cornelius was the same miraculous happening that had occurred on the day of Pentecost. This new happening represents the giving of the gospel to the Gentiles, who had previously not had the blessing of the good news. God demonstrates for us here as well as in other places that He is not a respecter of any person or race of people.

When the work we offer is supposedly for God and at the same time illustrates nothing but haughtiness and dogma, or ends with receivers who do not let it honor God, it is time to look at our motivation.

Transforming Will to Action

As I said earlier, it is possible just by *scanning the gospels* to understand that most, if not all, of Jesus' teachings have a flavor of removing external acts of religion to a worship that transforms the heart, mind, and soul.

'The Pharisees' religion was one of showing by doing, while their hearts were far from God, just as in today's world, what we call religion turns many away from Him. Why? I think it is because we are not living what we teach. Many do, and I'm well aware that they do, but the number is small in comparison to the whole. We must make every effort to internalize the nature of the Trinity, so that we are able to be God's messengers in truth and love. This is how the world can be won for Christ.

In the meantime, going back to the message of work, James says that work is necessary, as it serves the purpose of proving one's faith, but not as its motivation. Our motivation is love of God. What we do is proof of love.

How does this influential message of love manifest itself? As a person observes your relationship with God he might be moved to confide his need to you with questions or with an overture to friendship. This is where Timothy's admonition to be ready is useful: "Be diligent to present yourself approved to God, a worker who does not need to be ashamed, dividing the word of truth" (2 Timothy 2:15). Love demonstrates love, and those who come to know Him by the glory of the internal experience will demonstrate a changed life that will draw others to Him. This gives a twofold responsibility to both giver and hearer. To the giver, it continues the responsibility for giving out of love and concern to those who need. To the receiver, it indicates a responsibility to learn how to determine the accuracy of what you have been taught and to become ready for passing what you have learned to others who seek to know God.

I am prone to believe that knowledge begets knowledge, and that faith begets faith. This is because both knowledge and faith are addictive in the best possible way. This indicates the need for study and prayer, as the motivations that are most successful are nudges from within. Try it, and see for yourself. Blessings have a way of coming back to bless again, which makes it a marvelous tool. Let's make use of it often as we praise the One from whom all blessings flow.

The luxury and the beauty of life itself is a grand motivator for the praise we give to the Father. I know that we often compare our lives to those who have more and claim to be poor. Have you ever compared your circumstances to those who have less and seen the abundance of your riches? Be thankful, and in your conversation with God, ask God's blessings for those in need. Then seek out those who are in need and share that which can be shared.

Matthew says that works without proper motivation set up a "barrier" that is impossible to cross. I suspected from this that the barrier itself is multifaceted. Let's take a look at the reasons it might be so. First, the Jews and the Gentiles' attitudes toward each other were in and of themselves a barrier. I don't think it would be wrong to say that in general they didn't care for each other. Let's take a look at that before going on. Why was contention between them? 1) The Gentile homeland was given to the Jews to conquer (the land of Canaan, first known as the Promised Land). It made no difference that God had warned the Gentiles that their land would be taken from them unless they repented and changed their wicked practices. 2) Not only did He allow the land to be conquered by Israel, but He gave the Israelites a special law that was to be of great benefit to them. 3) He taught the Israelites to have nothing to do with those of the conquest who survived, but they didn't understand that it was to protect the children that would come from the inter-marriages between the two nations. These are at least some of the antagonisms that existed between them.

None of these problems would have burdened the Jew or the Gentile if they had been obedient and/or trusting of God, but the Jews who should have known better but didn't, continued to feel that God loved only them, playing the hypocrite, as if they possessed God's perfection when in reality they had no knowledge of forgiveness. The result was hardship on God's people. They forgot the love that came with the Oracles of God when they were entrusted with the Jews (Romans 3:2), and they became pompous and argumentative, and their love couldn't be found.

Few remembered the promise of the cross, yet some did. This was motivation to remain faithful, just as it is today. This is motivation to grow spiritually in order to be the best that we can be for our Lord. This is motivation to share the gospel with others because this is why we were created. This is spirituality, but first of all it is love because without love even spiritual growth is not pleasing to the Father. "Love covers a multitude of sin" (First Peter4:8).

Again from Chambers: "The great wonder of salvation is that His changes are heredity. He doesn't change human nature—He changes its source, and thereby its motives as well."[19] (Again date represents page in footnote.) As sinful beings, we need reconciliation with God, so by teaching spirituality, we learn from God instead of from Satan, but we have to really '*learn*' what we're hearing or we'll slip back into Satan's ways. An empty house will eventually be filled, whether by Satan or the Father.

---

[19] Oswald Chambers Assoc. Ltd., *My Utmost for His Highest Journal* (Uhrichsville, Ohio: Barbour Publishing, Inc., 1992), 7/24.

Fill your house with spiritual teachings from the Father, and make the transition from external religiosity to an internal faith that leads to change.

Observe the omnipotence of our God as your motivation. There is much to amaze that is visible in the universe—occasionally a glimpse of a planet, a falling star, the streak of an asteroid in the heavens, colors, clouds, stars, or beautiful trees within the planet to name only one of many items that could be named. There are motivations that need to be recognized within our houses, a roof over our heads, food to eat and clothes to wear, beds to sleep on water, lights and sewage. Most important of all there are usually children, sometimes a new baby to nurture. This is a blessing that keeps on giving, as some people say, and it should be that way, but the responsibility is yours, even though a lot of the problems may not be yours. That's life, and it doesn't help to say, "But that's not my fault." Life's not fair, so we go on with the best that is in us. God understands, even if no one else does, and really, He is the one who counts. Even the birth of animals is awe-inspiring, and how about the renewal of seasons? Has anything ever been as glorious? Perhaps grandest of all is the faith within that allows us to see God through the faithfulness of His believers. His works are beyond understanding, as are His accomplishments.

The question looms before us: "Of what benefit is our belief if, like the demons, we do nothing with it?" The answer to the question is, of course, no value at all. We have not shared our love of God and God's love for mankind, because we lack love. We are like a newborn who receives sustenance from the milk he is given but is unable to feed those around him. Allow your belief to become a proactive virtue that understands God's promises and that shows it by producing works by which to honor Him.

Such is the result of believing on the inside what was only done before externally. What was it God said? "I will put my laws in their minds and write them in their hearts And I will be their God and they shall be my people" (Hebrews 8:10).

I want to add just a few lines about the person who was always my mentor and my example. This person *knew* God. She was an avid reader but never read during work hours, not even the Word of God. She married for love, pure and simple, a "whither thou goest I will go, and whither thou lodgest I will lodge" (Ruth 1:16) type of person. She loved her husband with passion that took care of him. Though I never heard her say so, her motto seemed to be never to make him uncomfortable, never to make him wait for a meal, and always to have his clothes washed, ironed, and hanging in the closet, plus, if he wanted her to go with him somewhere she was always ready, or, she dropped everything to get ready.

How did he feel about all this? He adored her. They might go a couple of years without his buying anything for her, because money was tight, but when the drought was over, he added up everything he thought she needed (although she said she didn't need a thing) and bought it all. One Christmas, it was a brand-new gas stove, a set of silverware, and a beautiful dress from the best store in town, with a hat and gloves to go with it. New linoleum for the kitchen, wall to wall, was installed. There may have been more; this is what I remember.

Do you wonder why I tell you this? There's more. He always opened car doors for her, both in and out. He carried an umbrella for her and held it in case it sprinkled or rained. He wouldn't let her walk on the outside of a sidewalk, because someone might splash water on her. He insisted on taking that risk himself. They never said a cross word to each other, as far as I knew, although he teased her mightily.

Okay, so he was good to her, and she was good to him, but that's not exceptional, is it? Well, I'm not sure about that, especially in today's world. These are not the only reasons he loved her, though. She had a generous heart and took food to anyone in need, often bathing children and feeding them before she came home, along with maybe just a tiny bit of sorting laundry or sweeping the floor first. She made clothes for children who were pretty much in rags with her machine and left over scraps from other dresses made. She nursed sick people, and if you ask how she did all of this, it was that she was always up before dawn, with her day planned to the minute, and she never wasted so much as a straight pin or a piece of twine.

People came to her openly (or sometime in secret) for advice, and she mostly just let them talk, offering a suggestion here and there. They all loved her, as did we all. You may have guessed by now that this was my mother. She introduced me to teaching in the same way she did everything. She found a little group of children, largely in one family but with others added occasionally, and taught Bible stories to them all through the summer months. When the second summer rolled around she realized there were far too many children with too broad an age group for just one class, so she decided I could be her helper, and after some thought about it told me I would have what she called "the babies." She had to walk a little more than a mile to her class and pointed out to me that my stretch was only a half mile. So we began. This situation has always reminded me of hearing about children who were tossed into water and told to swim. I had never taught and was sure I would make a "bungle" of the whole thing, so I arrived at the place where the class would be and found that my 'group' consisted of one infant of the crawling stage in diapers, and three or four little girls (I don't remember which) for grades one, two, and three! I called it an initiation and the initiation was for me as a "teacher." I don't remember which story I told them, but they were all eyes and ears as they watched the baby and me. I bounced him for most of that first class and that was about all I accomplished, but they decided they liked it, so we kept the schedule for two months. After each class I would walk the weary half mile to home, Mother's class was always a little longer.

I gradually learned how to give these precious children few very short Bible stories and was even able to teach several little songs, The B-I-B-L-E was one The Wise Man Built His House Upon a Rock, complete with hand motions. Suddenly I was "teacher." From that point on, it was almost a second name—"Hi, teacher!" followed by a bounce or two and then, "Bye teacher!" On the playground at school, they would point me out to their friends and say "she's my teacher" and they'd argue about it until recess was over. There is nothing I've ever encountered that quite compares to a little girl's devotion. It is a precious memory.

I will close this little story by telling you that many years later, after my dad had died, Mother found a pulpit stand he had made—it was being used in one of the little churches she visited. She decided to stay there and she worshiped there until she died. She felt at home there because of that connection to him.

I mostly wanted to share this with you because as I thought about her one evening I realized that what I have learned about the spirituality of faith came from her example. She was very unprepossessing, caring, loving, and could find more ways to serve God than one could imagine possible. Of all the people I've known, my mother fits the pattern of one who set her mind on a course of spiritual action and then followed it. She studied and prayed as a matter of her life, not as a matter of religion. Going to church was an extra. It helped to sustain her through the week. It gave her notice of people she needed to help take care of, and occasionally it notified her of a function she wanted to attend, but *living* was her act of worship. The business of caring for people, helping to provide for them when she could, this was her nature, and it is the nature of God. And the nature I encourage us to practice in our day – to – day lives on this earth. She was a beautiful woman, but my problem came in knowing I could never meet the standards by which she lived. It was at her funeral that I finally realized it took her whole life for her to become who she was, and it gave me courage to keep trying. That's all God expects of anyone. To try and fail is not the same as to fail to try. He accepts us where we are.

9

External to Internal

Changing the Concept of Religion

The interpretative concept of the word 'religion' in the first century seems to have had a bearing on the manner in which the word has evolved and the meaning it carries today. When James wrote (about 49-50 A. D.) that a thing as small as the tongue could invalidate one's religion making it vain, he was telling them that religion was more than external, more than ceremonial display. Though the definition defines the word 'threskeia' as "ceremonial, an external process", there is a subtle change in spelling of the word (religion) when it refers to something that is pious. Then the spelling becomes 'threskos'. I am thinking that over the period of the past 2,015 years the wrong meaning has gained supremacy and our 'religion' became less pious and more 'external' even in matters supposedly pious in nature. The basic definition of religion didn't preclude piety in worship, yet it appears that the lower denomination of interpretation prevailed over any inward connection.

In retrospect, as we continue to study and learn it is possible to see that a large part of what Jesus taught in His three year ministry made reference to moving from the external aspect of religion to the internal aspect. Though it is seldom mentioned as such, the implication is there. James was not one to mince words. His letter to the Christians who were scattered throughout the known world, challenges Christians everywhere to be true to the religion that Jesus taught (James 2:8). "If you really fulfill the royal law according to the Scripture, "You shall love your neighbor as yourself," you do well." It was never called "external to internal," but much of it drew the conclusion that religiosity was not sufficient. We hear complaints from writers, speakers, presidents and more that sermons are not relevant, that the whole church thing is irrelevant. Why are our hands tied? We have the greatest story on earth and are bogged down by reasons that should be furnishing motivation.

To preach the gospel as it was done in the first century requires love, and we do it so timidly, not wanting to step on anyone's toes. To love God's people as He wants us to love requires faith and sometimes faith requires courage. Love that is demonstrated is capable of changing even those who think they do not love God. Remember the text that says, "As he [a man] thinks in his heart, so is he" (Proverbs 23:7). This is the only way to know God, and I must point out that it will no longer be external but internal evidence from the heart. Many theologians have said that knowledge of God cannot be proved by intellect. It is, however, proved by those who come to Him by the glory of the internal experience, which provides a changed life, for it is the changed life that draws others to Him.

There will be those who will say of the one who is so changed, "I knew him before, and he's nothing like he was then," meaning "He was like that, but now he is like this." This places our own internal knowledge of God on the same level as the knowledge of life itself. (I know, for instance, that I am alive, living.) I draw a conclusion, and as we incorporate the information, the Spirit continues to guide our hearts which are now open to the evidence as presented. It is from that moment that you will be granted the opportunity to *feel* the truth for which you have been seeking. It is a knowledge discovered from within. This provides greater evidence and greater enthusiasm for a lost and dying world.

Again from Tozer: "Proof lies in an invisible, unseen, powerful energy that visits the human soul, originating in the gospel. Such information needs no logic; it goes straight to the soul like a flash of light."[20]

You see, when we "do" for someone in need, in an attitude of love and humility, knowing that except for the grace of God that person could be us, we worship God. Of course, there are innumerable ways by which this

---

[20]   Tozer, *The Knowledge of the Holy*, 18.

can be demonstrated, but first, let me share a few experiences from some who have walked this path.

When we sit up at night with a person who is dying as we minister to the family, we worship God. When we teach with a kind and gentle heart, sharing what we have learned, we worship Him. When a father works all day, doing the best he is capable of doing for his employer, his family, and others, he worships God. When a mother prepares a meal for her family, she is worshiping. When a child is obedient to parents, teachers, or the government, he worships the God who provides all things. When a musician performs a concert or an artist creates a picture, God is glorified, because the talent came from Him. This is real-life "worship," and this is why Jesus included in His teaching the need to internalize heartfelt understanding that would be productive in saving souls. It is my opinion that the "watchers" always know the difference when they see "real Christians" or "Christians" who aren't real. Think about yourself when you meditate on this situation.

Many of the above examples go beyond the act itself. To illustrate a wider circle of responsibility, consider these as well. For instance, in regard to the workplace, a person must do the best that he can do for his employer, but his attitude about what he does also is very important—as well as revealing. A cheerful attitude, doing what must be done, or refusing to gossip or contribute to strife within the office, home, or among employees is a part of the getting-rid-of process that we seek in serving the Lord. Let the work of our lives reflect His glory.

In the same manner, let the entertainment of our lives reflect His purity, instead of the sinfulness of those who choose to follow Satan. If your work involves writing, music, painting, or any other art form, we must be careful to let the world see Him in what we create.

By going back as far as the Law, we can learn other important things in regard to internalizing the message. One, the priests didn't quite understand what they were doing by making daily and yearly sacrifices. They may have wrongly assumed that the act itself—which involved killing the animal, preparing it, and in some cases, cutting it up into pieces and making the offering—was the value of what they did. Perhaps the repetitive nature of the task had dulled their perception. At any rate they didn't *get* the internal nature of God's message—the part that involved mercy and grace.

There was no way Abraham could forget. For him, it was an act of unimaginable faith, because without knowing that God would not have him kill Isaac after all, Abraham obeyed God's instructions, maintaining the trust he had with God. Try to imagine the faith he exemplified in this action. Can you? By his trust, he gave to God a beautiful gift of love. As I try to understand the priest's failure to connect God's love for them with His obvious care and provision, as well as forgiveness (in spite of the fact that forgiveness was not a part of the Law), it seems to me that the ground was laid for their rejection in the first century. Perhaps memories overshadowed examples or perhaps the Israelites had slipped away from trust and had let their faith shrivel until it was no longer of value.

As for the Assyrian Israelites, who rejected the offer of repentance, one has to assume that this came from their satisfaction and enjoyment in living with the Assyrians. Sadly, it was less than a year before their country was destroyed. In 1 Timothy 6:10, we read that "the love of money is the root of all kinds of evil." They betrayed one of the first commandments by putting prosperity above the love of God. Assessing blame all these centuries later doesn't help us unless we take it as a warning and learn from their example. Both priests and rabbis drifted away from God because the more they argued, the more they forgot about love, and the more they misinterpreted Scripture. The bottom line was that they relied on themselves instead of on God. This is likely one of our problems as well.

Making It Possible

The most important piece of this puzzle is the Spirit. I've saved this for the last part of this section, hoping that the pieces previously received will help us to remember this part. These are the Spirit's most well-known visits to planet earth:

- Genesis 1:2. "And the Spirit of God was hovering over the face of the waters." *He was a part of the creation.*
- Exodus 35–36:1–2, Bezalel of the tribe of Judah was commended and chosen for the work of building the tabernacle. Then he was filled (1) with the Spirit of God, (2) in wisdom and understanding, (3) in knowledge and all manner of workmanship, (4) to design

artistic works, (5) to work in gold, silver, and bronze, (6) in cutting jewels for setting, (7) in carving wood, and (8) to work in all manner of artistic workmanship. In addition, He put in the heart of Bezalel and Aholiab and every other gifted artisan in whom He had placed wisdom who was stirred to do the work, to know all manner of work for the sanctuary. *He oversaw the work on the tabernacle.*

- Matthew 3:16. He was present at Jesus' baptism and appeared as a dove that descended and lit on Him. This is one of the few times we see the three together. *He was present at the baptism of Jesus.*

- Acts 2:1–8. "When the Day of Pentecost had fully come … Suddenly there was a sound from heaven, as of a rushing mighty wind, and it filled the whole house and they were all filled with the Holy Spirit and began to speak with other tongues, as the Spirit gave them utterance." *The Spirit was front and center on this important day.*

- Romans 12:1–2 gives both the why and the how His church was established. The how is as explained in the verse above. The why was because of sin. The Mosaic Law was designed to help the Jews recognize sin (by teaching what was right and wrong). In addition, it prepared them for the coming of the Messiah. Now His church begins where the Law left off, in order for spirituality to be taught. "I beseech you therefore, brethren, by the mercies of God, that you present your bodies a living sacrifice, holy, acceptable to God which is your reasonable service. And do not be conformed to this world, but be transformed by the renewing of your mind, that you may prove what is that good and acceptable and perfect will of God." This is both the how and the why. He wants us to have this indwelling presence to help prepare us for eternity and the work that awaits us in that new and incredible home. He wants us to learn, in the process of being guided by the Spirit, the *nature of what we are capable of when we worship Him in the midst of this life.* Also, through that transformation, we will be living proof of the character of God to the world around us. Having said that, I must add, "Wow! What a challenge!"

Setting Aside Desire

Desire is the negative side of motivation, but I do not speak of all desire, only of illicit desire, for which we find synonyms such as illegal, illegitimate, and prohibited. In James 1:14, we learn that each person is "tempted when he is carried away and enticed by his own lust." John gives further information. "Do not love the world nor the things in the world. If anyone loves the world, the love of the Father is not in him. All that is in the world, the lust of the flesh and the lust of the eyes and the boastful pride of life, is not from the Father, but is from the world, the world is passing away, and also its lusts; but the one who does the will of God lives forever" (1 John 2:16 NASB). It may not be obvious to you, but the verse from James is saying that this "problem" begins in the mind. The mind is the head of the body—the thinking organ, right? The mind tempts, and the body responds, and the mind is carried away. In a sense, it is a self-protective excuse inspired by Satan that says to his victim, "But I couldn't help it," whether it applies to lying, stealing, rape, or any other immoral thing.

Two important points to remember:

1. Temptation originates with Satan, but he always knows what to attack for the most effect. If your weakness is lying, he'll find just the right lie for the purpose at hand. If your weakness is stealing he'll tell you to go ahead—"The one from whom you steal has more than you have, and he'll never miss it"—and if your problem is sexual, he'll use his entire collection of excuses ("It's not that bad"; "God really made woman to be used"; "No one will find out anyway, and besides you deserve this. Go ahead, have your fun").

2. He is a mean, conscienceless being. He delights in pain and suffering. He has no morals, no empathy, and no compassion. If you wonder why he encourages sexual sin, it is because all other sin is in regard to *things*, but where there is sexual sin, he has broken two individuals—two strikes for one situation. Satan revels in self-contempt and pain. These are reasons he is said to be crafty.

The act of sin lessens our consciousness of sin and eventually causes us to quit caring about what others think. That is another way of saying it is addictive. As we continue in sin, in any particular way, the satisfaction in that sin decreases, and we seek other ways to gain the high we feel in an adrenaline rush.

You can learn the truth of this principle from smokers, drug addicts, alcoholics, serial-killers and even from those who over-eat. Over-eating or even sleeping can sometimes be termed an addiction if it holds one in its grip. This is why the inner man must cultivate the ability to live above the moral code of the day. It is a matter of self-protection and often the protection of those we love.

Making a Difference

Let's take a look at the things that make a difference between the external and internal displays of faith. I think most of us hate it when we *have* to do things. We are obviously too independent, because we don't really like to be told anything. It is perhaps just a symbol of growing up, or is it the same with everyone? Christianity, in some fashion, is something like being a parent. In the process of helping our children grow into responsible, caring, happy children, we are reminded of our own upbringing, which could be either a joyous or an unhappy memory.

We also talked about motivations that are destructive and how they raise barriers to personal growth. The only way I can explain such barriers is by concluding that it is more difficult for some people than for others to turn loose what has gone before. Of course, the Canaanites had been warned by God that unless they cleaned up their lack of morality and their idol worship, they would suffer defeat. So it is obvious that they believed the wrong people and did as they pleased. Here is what God said happened: "The Gentiles, who did not pursue righteousness attained righteousness, even the righteousness which is by faith; but Israel, pursuing a law of righteousness, did not arrive at that law" (Romans 9:30-33). Why? There is only one difference here—"because they did not pursue it by faith." The Gentiles proved their faith by putting it to work in their lives and internalizing it in their hearts. The Jews did not put their faith into action, because they did not believe it was necessary. The Law said it, and that was enough. Can you understand that by doing that they put the Law above God? They were actually following the letter of the Law but were not internalizing their faith. Jesus was their stumbling stone as they followed the path of their own interpretations. There is a tremendous lesson here for us. Do we do things for that reason? The sad thing is that being obedient is never enough. Hearts must motivate both self and others, and if they do, God forgives the lack of perfection in the gift itself.

I must point out that Bible study alone does not remove the veil between knowledge and spiritual perception. The old adage about a 'horse' applies here: you can lead a horse to water, but you can't make him drink. Just because one is led by the Spirit doesn't mean that guidance will be accepted. Guidance is the Spirit's work, but obedience is ours. Both are required for heavenly doors to open.

Please note in the above paragraph that both the Jews and the Gentiles were struggling over their own attitudes. These are the things that must be changed from within each of us. A changed life is the proof of a changed heart, which is why it is called transformation or metamorphosis. An amazing thing happens when it becomes "seen," in that those who notice the change want to know why you are different, and suddenly you have an invitation to share your life-changing story. Be ready to teach.

10

Self-Abandonment

Cleansing for the Lord

As we begin this list of things to do away with, I hope we can recognize that the church is called to live above the ability it possesses. No human can live spiritually in his own ability. The ability comes directly from God to the individual who is seeking. I have an idea that as individuals work together in His church, power is multiplied. This is certainly what happened at Pentecost, when about 120 people were enabled by the second day to teach three thousand. These three thousand became changed individuals, desirous of teaching others the gospel of Jesus Christ. This is the power of the Spirit!

The qualities in need of cleansing are basically attitudes that Satan has taught us and are the ones he encourages us to use plentifully on a daily basis. We never question how these sinful ideas get into our minds, yet we question how we will "hear" the encouragement of the Spirit. Both are spirits, and they both have the ability to penetrate the heart, the mind, the intellect, and even the personality. I suggest we give this serious thought. The Spirit's contact with man is *constructive*, whereas Satan's contact is for the *purpose of destruction*. Ridding ourselves of these sinful attributes is equivalent to a cleansing of the vessel. You and I are the vessels, and as we get rid of these sinful attitudes and habits, we are cleansed in preparation for the filling by the Spirit.

Before we begin the practice of removing these character disabilities, let me remind you that we hope to achieve a *changing* from a natural being to a spiritual being. This could be called "spiritual surgery," and if we called it by this name, we might feel the inner significance of the change we are looking for. It will not be easy. Here are some things I want you to remember:

1. *Temptation* is not sin. Jesus was tempted by Satan during His entire time on earth. Our Lord does not protect us from temptation, but He does provide the strength we need to say no.
2. *The preparation* required for this spiritual surgery, surprisingly, is not the same preparation you use to combat Satan. This battle will still be a battle in the war against Satan, but it also involves war against self. It is a difficult aspect to get our minds around; therefore, it will be the most difficult battle we will ever encounter. I say this because the nature of sin is not primarily immorality and wrong-doing but the nature of self that says "I am my own God." It is difficult to attack, because analyzing and knowing oneself isn't easy. We make excuses that we consider reasons; we procrastinate; and we compromise.
3. Try to remember this next point when you are in the midst of a decision. God makes us holy in the sense of *forgiveness*, which means that He no longer sees us in the blackness of our sins but in the purity of forgiveness. This implies a new beginning from the standpoint of *innocence.*
4. It is up to us, then, to turn that innocence into *holy character* by the choices we make.[21]

In addition, Oswald Chambers says, "The greatest characteristic a Christian can exhibit is unveiled openness before God, which allows that person's life to become a mirror for others."[22]

---

[21] Oswald Chambers Associates, Ltd., My Utmost for His Highest, character, 1/23
[22] Oswald Chambers Associates, Ltd., My Utmost for His Highest, openness. 1/23.

Selfishness

You may wonder how on earth we are able to abandon part of self. I'll agree that it isn't an easy job, because self is that self-centered, egotistical, stubborn, selfish, self-deceiving part of us to which Satan clings most tightly. Also, examining and excising self isn't a practice with which we are familiar. We seldom, if ever, see a need to give up a part of who we are. In fact, I would venture a guess that some of us are quite pleased with self. For example, a "humorous" conversation, generously salted with sarcasm can give the impression that one is witty but at the expense of the person under discussion. Or how about someone who "accidentally" lets the information "slip" that a certain friend was seen somewhere unexpected? Or in another scenario, a so-called friend belittles you by saying, "Put on a little weight there, haven't you, buddy?" These are somewhat minor examples, but if they are hurtful—if they create pain or hard feelings in any way—they are not of the Spirit. We allow selfishness to be on display in many ways. Let's look at another example of selfishness.

Covetousness

Jesus was asked to tell a man's brother that he must divide his inheritance with him, but Jesus refused and told the man instead to beware of covetousness. We might think that the one asking had a good point, and in our society today, the question might result in a law that forced the other brother to divide what he had. Jesus concluded by saying, "One's life does not consist in the abundance of the things he possesses" (Luke 12:13–5). Actually, the law contained many provisions by which family members would be cared for in the absence of money or possessions. Jesus knew the law, but He also could see inside the man's heart and realized that his motivation was greed and jealousy for what his brother had that he did not have.

Greed

The followng parable gives the other side of the story. A wealthy man was blessed with a plentiful harvest, and he worried that he didn't have room to store it, so he decided to tear down his barns and build greater ones in which he could store all his crops and his goods. Then he added, "Soul, you have many goods laid up for many years; take your ease; eat, drink, and be merry."

"But God said to him, 'Fool! This night your soul will be required of you; then whose will those things be which you have provided'" (Luke 12:19–20). The men of these two parables both showed covetousness and greed, but the bottom line was that they showed no love or gratitude to God for providing the harvest, nor did either brother demonstrate love for the other.

Lack of Self–Examination

Scripture teaches that selfishness takes many paths: hoarding, greed, indifference to those in need, indifference to sinners (failure to share the gospel), and self-indulgence. The need to examine self and following through with changes before they settle in and make themselves at home is of supreme importance. Many times, the discomfort of this process means we steer clear of this much-needed tool in our transformation. The ability to examine self in regard to motives and actions also is extremely important to self-cleansing.

Lack of Self–Abasement

We looked at humility under the heading of tools. Self-abasement is somewhat the same thing, only the examples in Scripture indicate a closer relationship between those who practiced the principle. For instance, Abraham bargained with God in regard to the destruction of Sodom, whose wickedness was such that God's intent was to destroy the city completely, but Abraham's compassionate heart prompted him to bargain with God over the possibility of saving the city if a certain number of righteous people could be found in the city. He did this very humbly not wishing to appear haughty or presumptuous. He began by saying "I who am but dust and ashes have taken it upon myself to speak to the Lord," and as the conversation continued, he said, "Let not the Lord be angry and I will speak." And yet again, "Indeed now, I have taken it upon myself to speak to the Lord," and one more time, "Let not the Lord be angry, and I will speak but once more." Because God felt compassion for the tenderness of Abraham's heart, He reduced the number required to save the city from fifty righteous to ten righteous. Unfortunately, even this small number could not be found, so the two cities were destroyed. Their names were Sodom and Gomorrah.

I confess that my relationship with God would not have allowed me to question Him even the first time. The very idea terrifies me. Think about this, because it shows how much further we need to grow in order to know God as Abraham knew Him.

John the Baptist said in reference to Jesus, "There comes One after me who is mightier than I whose sandal strap I am not worthy to stoop down and loose" (Mark 1:7). John knew he was doing God's work, yet in his humility, he recognized the one of whom he preached, Jesus of Nazareth, and would not claim any of the glory that belonged to the Son of God. His abasement was his own gift of worship to Jesus, the honor he offered to the one who was greater than he.

And then there is Paul, who said, "For I am the least of the apostles, who am not worthy to be called an apostle, because I persecuted the church of God" (1 Corinthians 15:9), and "that I should preach among the Gentiles the unsearchable riches of God" (Ephesians 3:8). Did you ever consider that Paul examined himself and found that he was guilty? Even though Paul had always prided himself on his obedience to and knowledge of God, he didn't hesitate to say, "I am guilty; forgive me, Lord." How often do we need to examine ourselves, but instead, we justify what we have done? These are examples of spiritual growth by self-abasement. I believe in time we will be able to see uses for this cleansing of ego. It is, in part, a matter of gratitude (or lack thereof) for talent we don't possess, (or do, but we consider another's work beyond what we are capable). I'm sure there are other ways to use this ability as we become more aware of it and as we grow accustomed to the need for our own self-abasement.

Excuses

The refusal in our society to take responsibility for our own actions is widespread. We justify our actions instead of taking responsibility. Further, we allow our children to do the same. There is a reason for consequences and reprimand—to teach and to train. Avoiding the responsibility of our actions is a harmful process that teaches by what we neglect to do. It teaches that there is no reason to follow moral and ethical laws, because preserving self is the ultimate goal in life. Thus, love of self is of supreme importance, over and above the needs of society. Natural law dictates that consequences follow every act, whether good or bad. Thus, the duplication of our self-preservation becomes our punishment. Society becomes what it has allowed itself to become through a lack of care—a society of disorder and conflict. Well-thought-out punishment that fits the severity of what has been done is a blessing.

Because this particular excuse was made at the time of the first sin committed on earth, we can assume that it is a favorite tool used by Satan. Adam said to God, "The woman whom you gave to be with me, she gave me from the tree and I ate." And the woman when asked why she had done this and she said, "The serpent deceived me and I ate" (Genesis 3:13 NASB). Neither Adam nor Eve was willing to take the responsibility for what they had done. What do you suppose Satan was doing at that time? I can see him smirking or chuckling as he tried to conceal himself in a tree, but God immediately spoke to him and told him of the curse he had brought upon himself. He would crawl on his belly and eat dust all the days of his life, and eventually he would be consumed, along with other sinners. Adam would have to earn his way by the sweat of his brow, amid the hardships of a sinful world, and Eve would bear children in pain and be under the rule of her husband. There are always consequences to actions.

In the parable of the talents, we have a different set of circumstances, where the first two slaves acted honorably and doubled what the master had given into their keeping, but the third slave buried his talent out of fear (or laziness) and could give back to the master only the one talent entrusted to him. His excuse: "Master, I knew you to be a hard man, reaping where you did not sow and gathering where you scattered no seed. And I was afraid and went away and hid your talent in the ground. See, you have what is yours," and he returned the one talent to the master (Matthew 25:24–25). "Throw out the worthless slave into the outer darkness; in that place there will be weeping and gnashing of teeth" (Matthew 25:30 NASB).

Excuses are contagious, and they are viral. The more they are used, the more they will be used. They contaminate relationships, misguide children, and weaken motivation. At the moment an excuse leaves your mouth, it brands you as a liar. I don't think we want to go there, because that's where Satan lives.

Laziness

This same parable identifies as "worthless" the one who didn't try. He was called lazy by the master when he returned and was thrown into outer darkness. This ending has a huge message. I suggest that we spend time meditating on what Jesus is saying. *Not to try is the worst thing we can do.* And then this wicked slave tried to justify what he did *not do* by blaming the master for being a hard taskmaster. The lesson here is plain: *use what God gives you.* He never requires more of us than we are capable of producing.

Indifference/Ignorance

And then there is that priceless parable about Jesus and the day of judgment, when He separates the sheep (obedient followers) from the goats (sinners), with the basis for the division being the benevolent deeds done for those in need. Speaking in regard to their eligibility to enter the Kingdom of Heaven, He makes six statements in which He states 'you did all of this for me" which His followers (the sheep) did for Him. He says "I was hungry and you gave me food; I was thirsty and you gave me drink; I was a stranger and you took me in; was naked and you clothed me; I was sick and you visited me; I was in prison and you came to me.'

And the righteous will reply when did we see you hungry, thirsty, a stranger, naked, sick or in prison and do these things for you?

And the King will answer "Assuredly, I say to you, inasmuch as you did it to one of these my brethren, you did it to me." And to those on

His left hand, (the goats) He said "Depart from me you cursed, into the everlasting fire prepared for the devil and his angels." The goats, you see had done none of these things and because they hadn't, they had failed to 'do for the Lord (Matthew 25:45–46). The lesson is quite clear. To do for our Lord, we must do for those in this world who are in need.

Principles of Judging

I saved one of our worst qualities for last. Don't you agree that judging is something we all do? Sometimes it's unthinkingly, but at other times it's in deliberate malice. I have tried to list these judgmental attitudes in specific categories to show what man is allowed to judge and which judgments strictly belong to God, and as you will see, there really isn't much that we are allowed to judge. Too often, we are guilty of misunderstanding the role of judging. I'm not claiming that I understand the two aspects perfectly, but I do know that all judgments are not the same. Let's take a look at the principles.

Judgment by God of the Unwise

"Do not judge so that you will not be judged" (Matthew 7:1-5). This is the verse with which many are most familiar. Unfortunately, our knowledge of this commandment usually ends there. The rest of the text gives reasons that judging others is unwise. "For in the way you judge, you will be judged; and by your standard of measure, it will be measured to you." The message of this warning is that God might have shown mercy, whereas you were unwilling to do so. Consequently, your own judgment in this matter will be without mercy. Instead you will be given the punishment you deserve, which is called justice. Unwise judgment is a dangerous choice.

Judgment by God of Outsiders

"What have I to do with judging outsiders … *those who are outside [the church] God judges*" (1 Corinthians 5:13, italics added). Let me point out that our responsibility with outsiders is to preach the gospel. *God alone is the judge of outsiders.*

Judgment by God of the Spiritual

"He who is Spiritual judges all things ..." (1 Corinthians 2:15). I can't, with any certainty, tell you what this is saying. My *guess* is that it refers to the one who has learned from studying the Word, from which he has discerned illumination and from which he may teach others.

And continuing the verse, "yet he himself is rightly judged by no one ... who has known the mind of the Lord that he will instruct Him [God]" (1 Corinthians 2:15–16). This suggests that no one is capable of giving a different interpretation, because God has already enlightened us on this subject, and no one is going to go to God and tell Him He got it wrong.

This doesn't imply that the Spiritual man, by reason of his "illumination," knows all things but that he knows what has been revealed, and that is the knowledge he is able to share. The phrase "judged by no one" likewise doesn't mean the natural man is incapable of recognizing the spiritual man's faults and shortcomings *but that he isn't able to judge* the accuracy of what the spiritual man shows him of a spiritual nature. Let me repeat the end of this verse one more time: "For who has known the mind of the Lord that he may instruct Him? But we [the one who is spiritual] have the mind of Christ."

We are plainly taught that such Spiritual insight does not come from the eye, the ear, or the mind but by the insight of the Holy Spirit. Such illumination is given to all believers who have the desire to know and is demonstrated by those who seek such knowledge. God allows this judgment in order that man's discerned wisdom, which is the wisdom that saves, can be shared with the "natural" man, who is an unbeliever. As for the one who cannot be judged, common sense should tell us that no man is perfect, and believers and nonbelievers alike are capable of witnessing the shortcomings of others, but we are *all* without the divine ability to evaluate the spiritual nature of the transformed. This word "all" includes the spiritually minded who judge each other. So the second portion of this verse refers to judgment that belongs to God. *God alone judges the Spiritually minded*, because this is where God *does* allow us—as *loving, faithful, obedient followers*—to make judgment on fellow Christians. We are given this responsibility for two reasons: (1) for the purpose of protecting the reputation of the body; and (2) in order to save the soul of the one who sins, who *may* be brought to repentance (1 Corinthians 5:1–5). Notice that each reason pertains to immorality.

Judgments by Followers

"Do you not judge those who are within the church? Remove the wicked man from among yourselves" (1 Corinthians 5:12–13). "If (you live) by the Spirit you put to death the deeds of the body and you will live" (Romans 8:13b). Notice the "if" in this verse, because *there is no other way the deeds of the body can be done away with, except by living in the Spirit.* Paul gives us more information regarding the deadly disease of immorality: "The mind set on the flesh is hostile toward God; for it does not subject itself to the law of God, for it is not even able to do so, and those who are in the flesh cannot please God" (Romans 8:7–8 NASB). Immorality within the church may be judged by believers.

The second reason for granting this responsibility, still connected with immorality, is found in 1 Corinthians 5:6–7. "Do you not know that a little *leaven* leavens the whole lump of dough? Clean out the old leaven so that you may be a new lump, just as you are in fact unleavened. For Christ, our Passover also has been sacrificed. Therefore let us celebrate the feast (Passover), not with the leaven of *malice* and wickedness (sin), but with the unleavened (pure) bread of *sincerity* and truth." (NASB, emphasis added).

Leaven is another of the symbols that represents sin. Christ was the Passover Lamb, sacrificed for the sins of the world, thus taking the place of the Jewish sin offering. Please note that the word "malice'" implies impurity of motive as well as the accusation of immorality. "Sincerity" in its Greek form implies an exact replica of the artist's model. It was actually a sculpting term that was given as a compliment for work rendered that seemed to be a perfect rendering. Here, it signifies that we are (in its ideal form) exact replicas of the sacrificed Jesus. I repeat: *Immorality within the church is the only reason a brother may judge a brother.*

These problems of immorality in no way justify the judging of other deficiencies of spirituality in other areas of one's life. God does not grade for severity; therefore, there are no big sins to compare against those that might seem smaller to the human nature. All sin separates us from the Father, who sacrificed His Son in order to achieve reconciliation.

There are at least two caveats regarding judging a brother. In matters of conscience, we are exhorted "to accept the weak in faith, *but* not for the purpose of passing judgment on his opinions" (Romans 14:1). Romans 14:10 adds the questions, "Why do you judge your brother … or regard your brother with contempt?" We are reminded that each of us will give an account of himself to God and should "determine not to put an obstacle or a stumbling block in a brother's way" (Romans 14:13). *Love resolves both of these cautions.*

Critical attitudes of contempt should be replaced with an attitude of concern and forgiveness, coupled with love. These critical attitudes and qualities must be abandoned in order to be pleasing to the Father. The very presence of these sinful conditions within the body is an affront to the presence of the Holy Spirit. It demonstrates again the impossibility for light to dwell in darkness, and it is the most obvious reason we remain in the flesh instead of having the ability to grow spiritually.

Spirituality of a Child

The topic of judging a child is a difficult one. Many factors enter in where a child is concerned. This stems from the fact that a child is dependent on the ones who care for him/her. There is a certain amount of knowledge, for instance, that the child doesn't possess, which must be a part of decisions. For instance, the child's trust, the naïve quality of that trust, as well as naivety of life in general are considerations that are easy to see. Love, patience, respect, and consistency are the mottos that should guide all dealings with children, because the parent is the child's security. A child should never be judged on the same level of knowledge as an adult. Remember, though, that any child will learn more from observing you and copying what you do and say than by any other method of teaching.

Before closing this section on self-abandonment we must first examine the principle that rests behind the empowerment of the Holy Spirit to accomplish the task that's been set before Him by the Father. For you and me it is quite possibly the most difficult abandonment we will encounter because it is the first, but also because it deals with the Holy Spirit, definitely an unknown quantity in our human existence. The principle is that contrary to opinion, we are not self-sufficient, awesome beings, capable of holding our future in our own hands as we tackle this complicated business of 'life'. It is true of us that we have become entrenched in the idea of self-sufficiency and hate to be told what to do or not to do to the extent that we are now many generations into being a people who subscribe to the theory of "Please Mother, I'd rather do it myself" even before that saying was a flippant utterance over our airwaves. To learn now that our Lord wishes us to "give ourselves to Him lock-stock-and barrel is rather a shock. The self-abandonment we are talking about is a relationship between God and man and even though man may seem to be self-sufficient he has many obstacles to overcome. God's offer comes with love which He has already proven. He wants to help you grow Spiritually, He wants to teach you where and how to find His blessings. I implore you to remember the part you play in this situation. It is with your participation in this step of abandonment, your motivation and your dedication that the Spirit will be able to achieve this monumental task. We (you and I) are in the position to be partners with the Holy Spirit just as in the world we are the ones who enable Satan in his evil work. The choice is ours, the success or failure is ours. We are capable with the Spirit's help to rid our lives of the wicked things introduced to us by Satan.

I was baptized when I was nine years old, and I will be eighty-two in March. I do so wish that we could accept this simple act of obedience without division in the world of Christianity. Just as a matter of common sense, we recognize that our knowledge comes to us differently. We see things differently, and our public worship has a different flavor. How could our continuum of understanding be identical? Why, then, must we have differences between us? I have several friends who were baptized in their seventies or eighties after having lived for God most of their lives. It was, I believe, a crowning achievement for them and beyond measure in the love that was gifted to the One who loves us beyond measure.

Baptism is a beautiful tradition and may quite possibly be the proof of love and devotion, instead of a reason for doing it. If so, it would be somewhat like Paul and James teaching about faith. Yes, we must have works but because of our love for God, not because the Law said we must. How is this controversy over baptism any different? If you say, "Because it is a matter of salvation" I will point out that the Jews thought the same in regard to the reason for their works, and Paul says they didn't achieve righteousness because it was not by faith.

We mustn't get so set in traditions that we can't hear the voice of God. I have always considered the verse in 1 Peter 3:21 of great value, that baptism is the "answer of a good conscience toward God." Faith is the reason for it all. Baptism is a gift of love and devotion and in return, we are gifted with the indwelling Spirit. I don't have the answer regarding how the 'timing' of such a gift affects the overall receiving of the Spirit, but my opinion is that the gift is granted at whatever point in one's life Lordship is recognized either by the individual or by God. God understands our confusion and knows either that the desire is in one's heart or the lack of such desire. I would like to add that it is conceivable to me that baptism doesn't *guarantee* the gift of the Spirit (which would depend on the heart), with the identical criteria for those who seek Him without having first been baptized.

11

The Spirit-Filled Life

Living in the Spirit

"The Spirit-filled life is not a special deluxe edition of Christianity. It is, however a part of the total plan for God's people."[23]

The Nature of a Spirit-Filled Life

"The Holy Spirit is a part of the Trinity who lives among and within us."[24] In addition to helping in the creation of the world, He does many lesser deeds of wonder, which have allowed me to think of Him as embodying such things as a mind, will, and personality. As for personal identity, I tend to think of Him as I do the Father and Son—as a person extremely deserving of honor—so I refer to Him using capitalization. Tozer says that in addition, He can rejoice, and He can grieve. While He does not have measurement, weight, height, color, or extension, he does have something He calls penetration, through which we are allowed to know God in a manner that is impossible intellectually. This is because we have the Spirit's guidance, plus the experience of "feeling," which allows our response to His urgings. If you have difficulty understanding the penetration of the Spirit, think of thoughts penetrating the mind or light

---

[23] Tozer, *The Knowledge of the Holy*, 18,
[24] Heschell, I Asked for Wonder, Signposts and Testimonies, 18.

penetrating darkness or air penetrating everything. The Spirit's penetration also transfers thought, as in Romans 1:18 (in order for man to know there is a God). And in Hebrews 8:10, there is the remarkable knowledge that His will can be written on man's heart, so that man can be pleasing to Him. This is probably the same penetration we refer to in speaking of the indwelling of the Spirit and His work within the physical body.

In case you have not considered this connection of the Spirit, let's take a look. It has been pointed out that whenever Jesus is *glorified,* the Spirit "comes." What does that mean? I think it refers to some aspect of the word itself; that is, a coming to the one who is *qualified* to be glorified. Say, for instance, that I am being baptized. I would not be the one to be glorified, which says that it is Jesus who is glorified *perpetually* for his sacrifice. Perhaps this would be a welcoming to Him of glory upon His return to heaven, as the angels sang in full chorus, or perhaps it is the glory He receives upon recognition of Him by the world. Whatever manner in which it is shown, it would be in Jesus' honor.

Perhaps most important of all is the glorification that comes to Him each time there is a new believer. After all, this was His reason for enduring the cross. It was His sorrow when those for whom He was sacrificed, ridiculed and taunted him, but it was His agony when the Father witnessed the sin of the world upon Him and turned away in grief. It was then that the agony of His suffering flooded His mind with love for the Father and He was once again glad that He was able to be a part of the Father's plan.

As I researched the 'come' words in the texts below I rejoiced in the promises of our Lord and God and it provided a change from the sadness of the paragraph above. I had not previously been aware of this information and it seemed fortuitous that it was revealed as I struggled with this idea of glorification which was also a new concept to me. I hope you will enjoy the change of pace it gives us and will rejoice with me in learning how Jesus is glorified, especially to learn that it was because one who had been a sinner is now a follower of the Christ.

The word 'come' can be used in three different 'senses' or ways in which understanding may be gained toward understanding the text. This is in part because the Hebrew language is fairly specific and allows such choice by the manner in which words may be combined, or as is more common by prefixes and suffixes. I will try to explain. The first two words (numbers 1 and 2) can reveal to the reader exactly how two angels would fulfill their assignments from God. For us, it tells us that one angel appeared in a dream while the other angel went in person and talked to the one to whom he had been sent as messenger. This means that this *could* happen to us if the circumstances required it! The third method refers to the second coming of the Savior (the Messiah). As you might expect, there is a wide variety of applications to choose from but fortunately these were identified by the Scripture used. Among the choices were "to come" or "to return" and "movement in space."

These are the three "senses" as used:

1. The angel may 'come' in a dream Genesis 20:4; or he may 'come' directly to the person, to whom God's has directed the message for a face to face conversation Judges 6:11.
2. God promises to 'come' to the faithful 'wherever or whenever' they properly worship Him; this seems to me to tie in with the giving of the indwelling Spirit (Exodus 20:24) partly because there is no restriction of time, and could apply to all ages. I'd like to add that on the basis of 'purpose' these events have a common denominator. Whether angelic messages of information or of warning, the guidance of Noah in building or filling the Ark, or the deliverance of God's people from Egypt, they were all essential pieces for the fulfillment of God's Master Plan. So whether His 'coming' saved the world from evil to further the plan, or the piece that would give Israel a place in which to become a nation of people who would be given a law by which to identify sin, and about the coming of the Messiah, it all fit together and was for the same purpose. The final example is more than likely the final one when again He will come for His people, this time it will be for the reward of faith. The sadness is that it will also be for those who choose not to be His people and for them there will be only punishment for rejecting His Son. I don't think I agree with that theory because the emphasis would seem to be on what God had done, not on the worship of the people and they didn't have control over the other issues.

3. The Hebrew for this 'come' translates "Bow" and is used to refer to the 'coming' of the Messiah (the Savior). There were other references that didn't seem to apply to this study.

How May we Hear Him?

How may we discern when the Spirit is within us? The answer is very simple: by usage. I caution you that you will not be able to 'call Him up' like a servant. Your procedure is to increase your interaction with God through study, prayer, and meditation. Through these moments, you will begin to hear/feel God's Spirit speaking to you, empowering you to change into His likeness. Consequently, a feeling of calm will comfort the soul. Urgings and "nudges" come to me, oftentimes when I am in the process of studying, researching, or hunting for something specific. Watch and listen for the Spirit as He works in and through your life, and allow yourself to trust His urgings.

Identifying the Spirit

What do we know about Him? Mr. Tozer calls Him a being and a person, and Mr. Heschel refers, as I do, to "Him." Heschel says, "We cannot make Him visible to us, but we can make us visible to Him."[25] As for personal identity I like to remember that He both laughs and cries which makes Him a warm, compassionate 'Him,' and I prefer to think of Him as well as of the Father and the Son in that way. Also as mentioned before, He has mind, personality and will and also, as discussed previously the ability, given our choosing, to penetrate our hearts, minds and souls. This choice allows the individual to learn from Him in ways that cannot be done intellectually. This is in part because of the experience of 'feeling' which allows us to respond to His urgings but it is also a matter of training to hear with the heart as well as with the ears. To most of us, these few brief technicalities in reference to the Spirit will not satisfy the hunger that pushes us to 'know.' The only satisfaction here is to understand that He

---

[25] Heschel, *I Asked for Wonder*, Signposts and Testimonies 18.

is with us by the grace of God and His desire is to benefit each of us as we prepare ourselves for eternity. If the Father had thought it would help, He would have gladly filled us in with all of the interesting details. Since He didn't, we are to assume it may have been more than our knowledge and understanding are prepared to handle, so in this as in everything, we should offer our gratitude and thanks for His loving care.

Receiving the Spirit

Actually there are quite a few ways in which the Spirit was received. At Jesus' baptism by John the Baptist, a dove descended from heaven and alighted on His head and a voice from heaven said "This is my beloved Son in whom I am well pleased" (Matthew 3:16 – 17). Of course, Jesus' baptism was to set an example for His followers, as well as to demonstrate the Father's approval in Him. Can you imagine the ability to see the Spirit of God in the form of a dove or to hear the voice of God as He praised His Son!

Pentecost was also unique in both purpose (the fulfillment of God's mystery by the establishment of the Church) and in method. The Spirit approached as a rushing mighty wind and descended upon the disciples who were waiting for word from God. Suddenly tongues of fire rested upon each of them and they began to speak in tongues. By this time a crowd had assembled to learn what was happening and each person began to hear in his own language. It was clear that this manifestation by the Holy Spirit was that for which they had been waiting. This, too, resulted in the glorification of Jesus.

In other situations the Spirit was received by the laying on of hands and by obedience of which baptism would be an example. Other examples such as Luke 11: 9 – 13 tell us of other ways in which one contacts the Spirit such as Luke 11: 9 – 13 which tells us

- *Ask,* and it *will be given*
- *Seek,* and *you will find*
- *Knock,* and *it will be opened*

And the conclusion: "if you, then, being evil, know how to give good gifts to your children, how much more will your heavenly Father give the *Holy Spirit* to those who ask Him?

The methods and the reasons by which Saul and Cornelius were contacted were quite different although the instructions received from the location to which God directed them was the same. That information—referred to as "the treasure"—meaning the gospel—had already been given unto human hands—earthen vessels—"that the excellence of the power may be of God and not of us" (2 Corinthians 4:7). This sounds like one of the reasons Israel was selected as God's chosen people. Do you remember—that God would receive the glory instead of the Israelites, primarily because Israel was the smallest of all nations without the power to accomplish what God would do.

The situations of the two men were very different in that Saul was a persecutor of the Church and God had to tell Him that He had been chosen to take that same gospel to the Gentiles (Acts 9:5 – 6). Cornelius' situation couldn't have been more different as he prayed regularly to god and was a generous man who gave much alms. Cornelius was seeking direction. Remember the text above "Seek and you will find?" Cornelius was actively seeking, and God directed him in a vision to a place where he could receive the information that he was seeking (Acts 10:4 – 6). As a result Cornelius and his household (relatives and friends) were all baptized and were gifted with the same manifestation of the Spirit that was given at Pentecost as proof that the gospel had now been given to the Gentiles (Acts 10:44 – 48).

On a smaller scale—but of no less importance—is the penetration of the individual heart that has occurred since Pentecost when we allow Him to be Lord of our lives. As we mentioned earlier this action on our part causes Jesus to be glorified. It is my opinion that the promise of baptism—the indwelling Spirit—implies the acceptance of the Lordship of Christ, as it also would when the Spirit is granted by request. If it did not include the same promise what would be the purpose for granting this blessing? That others receive Him by different methods and on different time schedules is a demonstration of His love for us and of His guidance. It is not a matter for our concern, except as a matter of rejoicing. Any person who has not given himself to the Lord by immersion misses that very personal demonstration of submission and should be allowed to do so. "Corresponding to that, the saving of eight souls—Noah and his family—and baptism now saves you, not the removal of dirt from the flesh, but an appeal to God for a good conscience through the resurrection of Jesus Christ" (1 Peter 3:21 NASB). *Accepting* the Lordship of Jesus causes the Spirit to come.

And finally, Paul questions the Galatians regarding how they received the Spirit. "This only I want to learn from you: did you receive the Spirit by the works of the law or by the hearing of faith" (Galatians 3:1-3)?

I think one of the best ways of understanding the Spirit is as one of the Trinity. Though they are one, I believe that they each have their own personality, their own way of doing their work perhaps their own way of thinking. However, they definitely seem to have different areas of responsibility. Our desire to understand remains, but thankfully, it is not a necessity. For me, there is a greater feeling of calm, understanding and peace to be aware of their connection with each other but also with us. It seems to me that from the perspective of each, Father, Son and Spirit, there has been a joyous collaboration to build this unbelievable home that awaits us. At this point in my life, I want to say that it feels like love on angel wings with our own personal 'helper' the Spirit of God.

Will We Recognize His Voice?

My own experiences have led me to expect to feel His urgings, although it is possible, as in one of the three senses of the word "comes," that He could be recognized through dreams. In my experience, our communication is more like a nudge of the mind, rather than a voice. It may be strange, but internal nudges are quite insistent. It almost always occurs as I study or after I have finished and have gone on to something else. Suddenly, the answer is there before me, and I have to spend some time with the feeling before I can go on. It's a great feeling. I don't talk about it, generally. Somehow, for me it is a very private matter, but I share now because good, honest, sometimes frightened people fear things they've not known and tend to avoid anything of that nature. This might be okay in certain situations, where a loving acceptance of our brothers in Christ must be maintained. Keep in mind, though, that Paul teaches us explicitly that we are to leave elementary principles and move on to the meat of the word.

C. S. Lewis says of man and God that it is the intimacy with God that allows spiritual growth. "The relationship between God and man is more private and intimate than any possible relation between two fellow creatures."[26] This indicates to me that there is a balance each of us must search for, one that fits who we are as well as who God wants us to be. Trust is the key; without trust, there will be little if any change within us, and the old facades will remain to thwart our longings to serve God in the way that would be most beneficial to us all.

In contrast to receiving the Spirit, which is God's gift, our part will require a lifelong desire to work, pray, and study. I say this because it will be a conflict of interest between the Spirit and Satan and a conflict of will between Satan and self. Of course, we must say (to ourselves and to God), "I will give up my will," and this is the goal, but by ourselves, it is impossible to do. Satan, by means of the will, is always nudging those he works against to go in the direction he wants to go. His way is never to our advantage. Remember Paul's statement, "For the good that I want, I do not do, but I practice the very evil I do not want" (Romans 7:19). If this was true of the great apostle Paul, it is certainly true of us. This means that the will is a major tool, either for you or against you, so you must take control of it.

"Present your bodies a living sacrifice holy, acceptable to God, which is your reasonable service" (Romans 12:1–2). The conclusion drawn from this passage is that a holy vessel is needed in order for it to be *filled with the Spirit*. That vessel is your body, cleansed of worldliness with His help.

We are unable to discern many things regarding the Spirit, but the more we think about Him, the more we will begin to feel Him, and it will be through this bonding of mind and spirit that He will reveal Himself to us, through the light of what we have studied and continue to study. In the meantime, let's try really hard not to limit Him by what we know. Leave the door open for more knowledge and understanding. This is the path to spirituality.

---

[26] C. S. Lewis, Margaret Feinberg *God's Voice Exposes* (Scotland: Thomas Nelson Publishers, 2011, 15.

12

The Progression of Faith

Faith Produces Faith

According to Peter's opening statement, Second Peter was written to "those of like precious faith with us by the righteousness of our God and Savior Jesus Christ" (2 Peter 1:1).

"His divine power has given to us all things that pertain to life and godliness, through the knowledge of Him [Jesus] who called us by glory and virtue, by which have been given to us exceedingly great and precious promises, that through these you may be partakers of the divine nature, having escaped the corruption that is in the world through lust" (1 Peter 2:3–4).

Imagine receiving this letter from Peter in the first century. There might be shouts of joy, "Our God has given us everything we need for life and godliness!" And another voice whispers in awe, "We will be able to partake of His divine nature!" And then shouts of praise echoes throughout the meeting place. "Praise Him praise Him, Glory to His name." Echoes of "Hallelujah" would come from all directions. Now imagine the same scene happening in a modern-day pulpit. The minister might call out, as the congregation rushes to the doors, "You might want to hang on here for just a moment. I know you're eager to get to the cafeteria, but we have a letter here from Peter." And as everyone disappears, he says, "Oh, well." And then, louder, "I'll post it on the bulletin board"—his voice trails off—"in case— any of you want to read it." He sighs.

Does this bother you? Of course, it is a created scene, but it hits too close to home for comfort. It sounds an awful lot like the after-service rush of today for the release of duty and a dash to resume life, having paid your weekly dues by sitting in a pew for an hour. Let's take a peek at what can be done on an individual basis, with decision, determination, devotion, and the Spirit of God.

This section tracks the *progression of faith*, which is the product of belief. It is also true that faith by the strengthening of faith produces more faith as does belief. Belief is one of the "non-negotiable laws" that God brought from the old covenant to the new. As we know, the new covenant had its beginning on the day of Pentecost, based on belief in the resurrected Messiah. The resurrection proved His identity as the Son of God. The followers of this spectacular faith quickly grew from the 120 followers who were present at the miraculous beginning to three thousand by the second day. It is estimated to have reached tens of thousands across the known world before the end of the first century. As love develops into faith, it becomes an *active faith*, which, as James says, is *proof* of our belief. It is this active faith that sets the stage for spirituality and, by so doing, enables His followers to partake of His nature.

Peter writes to followers who are scattered by the dispersion to explain to them how they are to attain these blessings. In his introduction, he tells his readers that by giving them this information, God has given them "all things that pertain to life and godliness" and that all of these things come through knowledge of Him. Wow! I almost feel this is something we should memorize or put in a place where we can easily see it every day. It says to me both *why* we do as we do and *how* it can be done. Do we really get that? Peter is saying, its' all here, you don't need anything else'. That, my friends, means that we are likewise blessed. Let's take a look then at what we need.

Pattern for Progress

Add to your faith virtue—How perfectly appropriate that Peter begins his list of virtues with faith, which is the product of an active belief. Let me share the depth of this little word "add." It doesn't just mean "add virtue to faith," and make your group bigger. It implies that we are to give lavishly and generously. The question is, "What are we to give?" It begins with giving ourselves, and Peter has already said that we are to give "all diligence to add."

This phrase takes us back to another phrase, "pursue righteousness." Why do we use the word pursue? 'Pursuit' informs that it is an urgent mission as does the idea of diligence. What exactly is virtue? In classical Greek, virtue meant "the God-given ability to perform heroic deeds."[27] This is not surprising, considering the emphasis the Greeks had on building the physical body and on athletics. It never meant to them a cloistered virtue or attitude, but virtue that is demonstrated in real life. It later came to mean "that quality which made someone stand out as excellent."

Paul is perhaps speaking here of *moral* energy, the voluntary power that performs deeds of excellence for God out of the motivation of love. In that case, virtue is very much a part of this thing we have called religion. While virtue is not necessarily connected to religion, this motivation would place it there. The root word for virtue is *worth*.[28] *Its definition is "that substance or quality of physical bodies by which they act and produce effect on other bodies." The 'other bodies' I believe in this case would be those who accept the gospel; the worth would be the one who is teaching, either a person or the Spirit Himself. Let me explain. A chemist would speak of the virtue of a certain plant in medicines or drugs, and it would be interpreted as its worth or its value, which would be measured by its strength. This, then, would be "that quality that makes a thing useful." The third definition of virtue (which we would have expected to be the first) tells us that virtue is "moral goodness," and a little later, can be found this addition: "the value of mental qualities, useful, excellent." The bottom line, I think, goes back to the Greek translation: virtue is the value of and the worth brought to, your spirituality.*

By combining the outstanding words "power" and "strength" to the root word "worth" we have "that substance or quality of physical bodies

---

27 MacArthur, *MacArthur Bible Commentary*, 11.

28 Noah Webster, *American Dictionary of the English Language, 1828*, Copyright 1995 by Rosalie J. Slater, (republished in facsimile edition by Foundation for American Christian Education, San Francisco, CA, 1967), permission to reprint the 1828 edition by G. & C, Merriam Co., Eighteenth Printing, 2006, W: worth, V: virtue.

(in this instance, this refers to the spirituality of Christians, as the substance within) by which they act and produce effects on other bodies *(this refers to the influence of spirituality on others)*, and we have discovered the worth (or the value) of living by the Spirit. It is no longer surprising that Peter added virtue to faith at the very top of the list in the progression to spiritual maturity.

Add to your virtue knowledge—Lets' take a step back and ask of what value or worth does Jesus affix to us as Christians? We know instantly why Peter is taking us to knowledge. As we spend more time with the Spirit, He "reveals" the nature of Jesus to us, allowing our knowledge to be more intimate, broader, deeper, and more accurate. It is a knowledge based, for our part, on repentance, with the faith to sustain.

The Christian faith is built on truths. They are not truths of the world, but truths of God. God desires that we have understanding of these truths so that our insight of them will demonstrate their "worth." The proper insight of these truths will lead to an *applied* faith that will bring others to Him. In this way, we are His messengers. This requires diligent study and pursuit of truth in the Word of God. John MacArthur states that Christianity is not a "mystical religion, but is based on objective, historical, revealed, rational truth from God and intended to be understood and believed. The deeper and wider that knowledge of the Lord is, the more grace and peace are multiplied"[29] (2 Peter 1:2). Knowledge is the guidance received by the Spirit, and one of the ways He speaks to you is through God's Word.

Add to knowledge self-control—First century, athletes were expected to be self-disciplined, and it was from that experience that they learned to maintain self-restraint. Self-control literally means "holding oneself in." The implication for a Christian is that he must control the desires of the flesh with its resulting passions and maintain control over his body. By combining what we have so far, we can see that virtue (strength, worth) guided by knowledge (understanding of God's truth) is necessary to learning self-discipline over the desires of the flesh. The desired result is to make the flesh the servant instead of the master.

---

[29] *John MacArthur, The MacArthur Bible Commentary,* knowledge, 1927, 2:1.

Add to self-control perseverance. Perseverance — in theology — means "to continue on in a state of grace to a state of glory."[30] This is also a perfect definition of the words "complete" and "perfect" as they are used in Scripture; grace must be maintained while living in order to exchange that grace at the time of death for glory. The word perseverance is sometimes used as a substitute for patience or endurance and carries with it the idea that one doesn't quit for any reason. The martyrs of the first century and in today's world who practiced perseverance understood this principle and practiced it. It is the staying power that embodies hope.

Add to perseverance godliness. To be godly is to live in obedience (Jesus was obedient to the point of death) and have reverence for the Father, Son, and Spirit (always mindful of the Creator because of who He is, because of what He does, and because of His love). "And now abide faith, hope, and love, these three; but the greatest of these is love" (1 Corinthians 13:13).

And to your godliness add brotherly kindness. I used to wonder if Peter was speaking here of kindness to those within the church, and while *kindness* is a fruit of the Spirit, it is not limited to those within the church. I do believe, however, that *this* virtue gives special emphasis to brothers and sisters in Christ. "Let us do good to all, especially to those who are of the household of faith" (Galatians 6:10). It is very possible that this admonition carries an even deeper meaning in the sense of mutual sacrifice and love. The term "brotherly kindness" is only used twice in Scripture, both times in First Peter 1.

And to brotherly kindness add love. Love, I believe, is the achievement of all the virtues. "If these things are yours and abound, you will be neither barren nor unfruitful in the knowledge of our Lord Jesus Christ. For he who lacks these things is shortsighted, even to blindness, and has forgotten that he was cleansed from his old sins. Therefore, brethren, be even more diligent to make your call and election sure, *for if you do these things you will never stumble*; for so an entrance will be supplied to you abundantly into the everlasting kingdom of our Lord and Savior Jesus Christ" (2 Peter 1:8–11, emphasis mine). This verse is a great example of needing to find other texts to understand it. I wouldn't like to leave you with the idea that you can reach the point where you no longer sin. "You can never stumble"

---

[30] Noah Webster, *American Dictionary of the English Language, P* : perseverance

could leave that impression, unless you know there are other passages that teach otherwise. I think this phrase is an explanation of the result of temptation and even of sin, and repentance provides the guarantee that you will not fall as a result. Repentance is always the key.

The Nature of the Spirit-Filled Life

How many books have been written on the subject of love? I doubt any of them have covered it as well as Paul did in the thirteenth chapter of First Corinthians. The gentleness felt by reading this chapter soothes but also challenges and prods. I heard a man by the name of Scott Peck speak one time, probably on the subject of love, because the quotation I jotted down was definitely on that subject. Here is what he said: "Love is the wheel by which we extend ourselves for the purpose of nurturing one's spiritual life." It struck me as a very apt description of how love flows between us, especially in the absence of any overt demonstration. The idea continues to intrigue me that we are aided in this way through our relationships with the Spirit.

To the measure that we are successful in cleansing and preparing our vessel, we can expect the Spirit to begin our filling, even as we learn. What is "new" within will enable additional spiritual growth, and we will experience an unexpected peace in our new spiritual life in Him.

Walking in Love

Love fulfills. When Christians genuinely love, they fulfill all of the moral commandments of the Mosaic Law and demonstrate the "ruling principle" of Christian freedom (love) (Romans 13:8).

Love edifies. To edify means to instruct or enlighten. This must be done in such a way as to encourage and build one up in Christ (1 Corinthians 8:1).

"Love suffers long and is kind. Love does not envy. Love does not parade itself, and is not puffed up" (1 Corinthians 13:4). I see this verse as describing two different types of people: one who is not easily offended and is kind to the persecutor, and one who is full of self and always makes an attempt to be the center of attention.

Love "does not behave rudely, does not seek its own, is not provoked, thinks no evil; this person, conducts himself politely, thinking of the comfort of others before his own, is willing to let others be 'first,' and keeps a pure mind" (1 Corinthians 13:5).

Love "does not rejoice in iniquity, but rejoices in truth." Iniquity here could refer to several things. I would consider it to be any expression of wickedness, perhaps even a secret joy prompted by another's failure in some way, in which case the iniquity would belong to the one who is lacking in love. As for truth, this person doesn't participate in deceitful practices (1 Corinthians 13:6).

"Bears all things, believes all things, hopes all things, and endures all things." This person has broad shoulders on which he takes responsibility, believes in the future, and doesn't complain (1 Corinthians 13:7).

"Pursue love." Pursuit is the act of striving and definitely conveys the idea of an active participation. This is not speaking of romantic love but an attitude of love, a method of dealing with all situations, perhaps in particular situations that are difficult—a "do unto others" type of response in which you defuse anger and frustration (1 Corinthians 14:1).

"Love serves." This verse is a challenge to followers of the Lord to pattern self after Jesus, who came to this world to *serve, not to be served.* (Galatians 5:13).

"A friend loves at all times." A friend is steadfast and dependable (Proverbs 17:17).

"Love your enemies, bless those who curse you, do good to those who hate you, and pray for those who spitefully use you and persecute you." This is the manner in which Jesus treated those who hated Him (Matthew 5:44). As I've said, He does not ask us to do anything that He has not first demonstrated in His own life.

"Love one another as I have loved you." The first meaning of this kind of love is that we must give ourselves to Him. In order to do that, we must first die to the desires of the flesh. After that, we are to love each other to the extent that we would give our lives for them as Jesus did for us (John 13:34).

"Do not love the world or the things in the world. All that is in the world—the lust of the flesh, the lust of the eyes, and the pride of life—is not of the Father, but is of the world" (1 John 2:15–16). These verses are also a foil to liberty as they challenge the believer not to use the freedom of the new covenant in order to sin but to make choices wisely.

These are twelve of the ways in which we can begin to work on ourselves (through proper application and love) in order to know that the love of God dwells in us. I have no doubt it is a partial list, and that as we grow we will find other ways of expressing His love that so richly blesses us each day. As our love develops, growing stronger in each aspect of responsibility, I believe that beyond being found pleasing in the sight of the Spirit, we also serve as a sort of enrichment for Him, by the reward of our spiritual growth that glorifies Jesus. The Spirit, then, in reality is the reason Jesus is glorified, because He is our teacher, our guide, and our helper in all ways. Our obedience to His guidance informs Him of our desire to continue to grow in the effort to become more as He is.

Walking in Joy

This joy is not that which welcomes one home from a distant land, or the joy of a child's birth; or the joy of one who has escaped physical death. It is the joy of a sinner who repents and returns to the fold (Luke15:7; Luke 5:32; Mark 2:17).

John speaks of the joy that comes from "abiding in God's love," which is another way of saying that "he keeps the Father's commandments" (John 15:10–1).

John speaks of the joy that Jesus experiences with the Father in their *unity of purpose*, especially for the faithfulness of the "eleven" given to Him by the Father, and he prays that they may experience *a like joy* as they go to the world, knowing that the world hates Him and therefore hates them. He asks God to keep them safe from the Evil One.

Paul speaks of joy as a fruit of the Spirit, which is added to love and which enables peace.

Paul proclaims to the Thessalonians that they are his hope, his joy, and will be his *crown of rejoicing* at the time of their mutual presence at the coming of the Lord Jesus Christ (1 Thessalonians 2:19–20).

James, the brother of our Lord, is quoted as saying, "My brethren, count it all joy when you fall into various trials." Why did he say this? Because he had the knowledge of experience that it is testing that produces patience, which leads to the "perfect and complete" man of God (James 12:4). James was later beheaded by the Roman government for his faithfulness.

Peter, again exhorting those of the dispersion to rejoice in suffering for Christ, "that when His glory is revealed, you may also be glad with exceeding joy" (1 Peter 4:13).

Joy, as we have witnessed from these verses, is a quality that has strictly to do with *faithfulness* and *salvation*. It does not mean that our lives from day to day should not be joyful; quite the contrary, as we will understand when we examine the virtue "peace." However, it is my opinion that the joy of these verses, as they apply to the spiritual, is *for the purpose of applying focus.* If we are able to master the principles of joy in regard to spirituality, the things that are natural to our humanity will certainly follow.

Walking in Peace

"I did not come to bring peace, but a sword" (Matthew 10:34). This verse explains that this seemingly strange statement is meant to separate us from anything that would prevent our putting God first in our lives. While the ultimate goal of the gospel is peace with God, He would not have us believe that our lives will be free of conflict.

"Peace and goodwill toward men" (Luke 2:14). This is the song the angels sang at the birth of Jesus. Since man's peace with God is dependent on man's justification, one must remember that God's peace is for those on whom His pleasure rests, referring again to the act of justification.

Peace rejected will be hidden. Jesus chastised the Pharisees for not recognizing the things that would have made their peace, "but now they are hidden from your eyes" (Luke 19:42), illustrating His rejection by the Pharisees and their failure to repent, which would have brought justification to them and contact with God's grace. We must remember that opportunities do not last forever.

Jesus said, "My peace I give to you; not as the world gives do I give to you. Let not your heart be troubled, neither let it be afraid" (John 14:27). This verse shows the heart of God's peace, *the knowledge that He will return for us.* "Don't worry about anything," He says. "It's all taken care of." What is our responsibility in this matter of possessing His peace? *Our responsibility is to remain faithful and to be ready.*

"Having been justified by faith, we have peace with God through our Lord Jesus Christ" (Romans 5:1). This little verse always reminds me that God has put away His wrath against those who believe and obey.

"He Himself is our peace, who has made both one, and has broken down the middle wall of separation" (Ephesians 2:14). Here, He speaks of the abolishment of the law, which had been a point of contention between Jew and Gentile but as a result of the resurrection is now removed, creating "one new man from the two, thus making peace."

The peace of God which surpasses all understanding will guard your hearts and minds" (Philippians 4:7). Paul refers to God's peace as the protection that keeps them safe; this is a *spiritual protection* that assures that physical death is not the enemy.

Paul tells Timothy that peace, along with righteousness, faith, and love, is to be pursued (2 Timothy 2:22). To be pursued means that *these virtues are not left to chance.* Pursue is an active word. Seek and find what you seek.

These are the ways in which peace blesses our lives. I have come to think of the word peace in its scriptural sense, as confidence in God, which means that I trust His promises. The challenge to be ready when He comes for us implies total faith in His atoning blood, which removes any doubt or fear and results in peace through the knowledge of Him.

Walking in Patience

Patience as a virtue implies "calm endurance" or "tolerant understanding," which denotes tolerance over a period of time. In the parable of the sower, the seed that fell on good soil required time to produce a crop. The symbolism here is that the one who heard, having a good heart, had patience. He did not expect an immediate return and, in time, was rewarded (James 1:3). "The testing of your faith," James says, is what "produces patience."

Then James takes it from the symbolic to the real by saying, "Let patience have its perfect work, that you may be *perfect and complete*, lacking nothing" (James 1:4 my emphasis added). Another way of saying this is that this isn't going to happen overnight. Give it time to accomplish its purpose. God has promised that when we are presented to Him by His Son, we will be declared perfect. He has also defined that moment as being complete, letting us know that He speaks of the judgment. In Revelation 1:9, John tells the churches, "I'm not only your brother in this tribulation [the persecution of the saints], I am with you in His kingdom and in the *patience of awaiting His return*" (emphasis added). He was, in fact, giving the churches his credentials, his right to speak to them of God's message. It is wise to remember that God's kingdom spoken of here is the church, the kingdom on earth. In time, the earthly kingdom will be united with the heavenly kingdom, and we will be one, which is still a future event.

I would remind us, as we wait on the patience of the Lord for the final day of reckoning, that we have much to do to occupy ourselves. As we turn our attention back to the virtues that teach us of God's nature that are necessary for our spiritual growth. I hope we are reminded that the best thing we can do as we wait for that awesome day is to be prepared.

Walking in Kindness:

First I would like to know if this kindness is any different from the term "brotherly kindness." The answer is that in the Old Testament there was some difference, as it referred to God's long-suffering love—"His determination to keep His promises to His chosen people in spite of their sin and rebellion" (Deuteronomy 7:12). While it evidently is not used in this context in the New Testament, that does not mean that Christians do not cause long-suffering for Him. The responsibility for asking for repentance, however, falls on our shoulders. In addition, we are urged to be kind to all, but "especially" to those of the household of faith (Christians, followers of Christ) (Galatians 6:10). An example is the command to distribute to the needs of the "saints" (again, this refers to those who follow Christ) (Romans 12:13).

Paul, in Ephesians 4:32 gave a good description of kindness. As we deal with one another, we are to be "tenderhearted, and forgiving even as

Christ forgave you." Again, I would add that this text involves the principle of doing unto others as you would have them do to you.

If we always act in kindness, we avoid giving offense to others, thus preventing blame from falling on the ministry (2 Corinthians 6:6). At the same time, such action is designed to bring glory to the Lord.

And the final admonition from Hebrews 13:1—"Let brotherly love continue." Let me point out that this last chapter of Hebrews contains only twenty-five verses, and they all express a form of spiritual growth. Try reading it from that perspective.

Kindness is such a simple word and seems such a simple command. Why do we need help to understand its meaning? I wonder, and yet here it is, so it must be something that *generally* we are lacking. Matthew says that kindness is "a tender concern for others reflected in a desire to treat others gently" (Matthew 11:28–9).

Goodness is manifest by kindness and carries the meaning of moral and spiritual excellence. The Spirit causes this goodness to be manifest in our nature, even though "there is none good" except God. Yet we are to manifest this goodness of God.

Faithfulness means loyalty and trustworthiness (Philippians 2:7–9). These verses demonstrate the faithfulness of our Lord Jesus. "The Lord's loving kindnesses indeed never cease, for His compassions never fail. They are new every morning, great is your faithfulness" (Lamentations 3:22–23 NASB). I feel this verse provides a little more insight into the idea of compassion.

Gentleness (the King James Version and the New King James Version translate this as meekness)—an humble and gentle attitude that is patiently submissive in every offense, with no desire for revenge. In the New Testament it is used to describe three attitudes: (1) submission to the will of God (Colossians 3:12); (2) teachability (James 1:21); and (3) consideration of others (Ephesians 4:2).

Self-control must be restrained over passions and appetites. Basically, I realize this is the primary thrust here, but I would like to add the idea of learning restraint over emotions for the purpose of dealing with children, those who are ill, family members, etc., 'Time' needs to be correlated with 'activities' and with time for study and meditation.

These nine "fruits" are the ultimate goal for which we must work. Paul concludes this list of things by adding, "If we live by the Spirit, let us also walk by the Spirit. Let us not become boastful, challenging one another, envying one another. If anyone is caught in any trespass, you who are spiritual, restore such a one in a spirit of gentleness; each one looking to yourself, so that you too will not be tempted" (Galatians 5:25–26; 6:1 NASB).

The very idea of being filled with the Spirit is a mysterious concept—it is a mystery as to how it is accomplished. One of the first things I learned about the Spirit was that it is an either/or situation. "Do not get drunk with wine, for that is dissipation, but be filled with the Spirit." I accepted the concept itself of being filled with the Spirit, but I've found there is more to it. It just doesn't make sense that there would be no filling until the vessel is completely filled. As we learn, the Spirit begins to fill our vessel with the knowledge we are able to handle, and it will continue in that fashion as long as we continue to change in what we know and what we are able to use.

It is possible that the text may refer to the ideal rather than the process. We will never know exactly how the Spirit accomplishes His work, but I am so thankful that He is our guide. Don't forget that His changes within us are dependent on our desire to grow spiritually. Our prayers could begin with, "Oh Lord, help me to know, help me to see, and don't allow me to make excuses." This is how we can make preparation for Him. The *wanting* signifies our desire as our *striving adds virtue* (strength, value) to what we do. I feel, as with anything else done for the first time, that repetition will improve the quality of what we want to accomplish in ourselves, as well as in our efforts to pass the "illumination" on to others.

I think of these virtues and fruits as developing in sequential order, but I'm quite sure they overlap. Our lives have to change, or else all the knowledge in the world will not let the light of God shine through. As I have tried to illustrate, living by the Spirit is not just a matter of being filled. We must also be emptied of all of Satan's "self-isms" from which our own concept of self-realization derives. Our work, as you can see, is cut out for us.

This doesn't mean that we must wait until we are completely emptied and filled before we can begin our walk with Him. This is another reason

I don't believe the concept that illumination is an instant process, which would be like saying a baby must be able to walk, feed itself, use the potty, and read and write before we allow him association with the family. That is just wrong, and it is amazing how like the family God created His plan. Do you wonder why? I think it was because the principles of His plan work whether it is in the church, the family, businesses, or government. He knows and understands man's nature, yet in spite of how bad our basic nature is, He loves us. Please remember that Spirit-filled people are changed people. If you can't quite decide where and how you have changed, you may need to do some self-examination. My own evaluation of self occurs daily, and I'm hard on myself because I can see and feel ways in which I should have progressed. In all honesty, I find myself still taking baby steps in that particular regard. The will is an amazing tool when it becomes activated.

Another thought to keep in mind is that lack of obedience will quench the Spirit within. Set your heart to a more passionate desire to strengthen your relationship with Him. We have the record of how the first Christians grew; study it and contemplate how the New Testament faith produced so much, and then live it.

13
Putting it Together

As We Live in the Spirit

I have called this study *From Faith to Faith* because it is a continuation of learning that began with what we call first principles. Many followed that call, and many have grown into pillars of faith, with unlimited motivation and vision for the future. Many have not been that successful, and thousands, perhaps multiple thousands, have remained where they were when they accepted the call to follow the Savior. I believe the single most prevalent roadblock that prevents us from growing spiritually is *our own reaction* when we hear the words of Jesus saying, "If anyone wishes to come after me, he must deny himself and take up his cross and follow me" (Matthew 16:24). Our minds immediately give us Satan's interpretation: "Oh, but He doesn't really mean that. You are just misunderstanding Him." Remember the Garden of Eden? I recently read another interpretation of that verse. It is very blunt. It reads this way: "If you want to be my disciple, you must give up your right to yourself and give that right to me." You have to admit there is an appeal to believing Satan's lie, and on what "I" want, but God demands that we put nothing or no one before Him.

The comparison of Colossian 3:5–8 lays out the roadmap of continual, progressive "putting on and putting off." This is the point at which we need to pick up our lives for Him, rejuvenate them, and be transformed by the renewal of our minds. The fact is, we can only achieve that goal if we launch forth and *become* what God has granted us to be. This allows the world to see only Him as the giver of life. The challenge is before us. Any spirituality gained will fulfill His command to "Feed My sheep." It isn't so much what we do as the motivation of *why* we do. This is the reason our attitudes are so important. Do others see Christ in us? Are we giving others the love Christ gave for us on Calvary? It is only after the inner man becomes visible that we will be seen as belonging to God. Until then, depending on attitude, what we do is often busy work, instigated by our own initiatives. When we love Him, the Scripture will be fulfilled that says, "Let your light shine that others may see your good works and glorify your Father who is in heaven" (Matthew 5:16).

It is my opinion that we do not intentionally grieve the Spirit. We do not intentionally sadden the Father or neglect the Son. These are not actions that we set out to do. To the degree that these problems are not intentional, they say to me that there is a solution. It is my prayer that we will understand the gravity of our situation and find a way in which we can implement it by a course of action. I believe with all my heart that as we begin to serve Him (in the sense of gaining spirituality), that unknown to us, He is at the same time transforming us into the new persons we seek to be. When this happens, we will know that belief, faith, and spirituality are no longer abstracts in our lives because the visibility of change will have energized those heavenly qualities and removed any abstract quality they once had. Our God is truly amazing, isn't He?

I pray that you have benefited and will continue to benefit as you hold this message in your heart. *From Faith to Faith* has been very special to me. Working on a project that involves a miracle-like metamorphosis has been an inspiration for me that will enable future work, God willing. This sometimes beautiful, sometimes tragic life will someday be over, but even better, it will be "complete," having been "faithful unto death." We will have the privilege of living in the heavenly realm in His presence, with no more tears and no more sorrow, with all things provided. What a blessing!

As you continue your growth in spirituality, don't forget that grace and peace are gifts that spring from virtue and knowledge, that virtue is a mark of excellence, that self-control and perseverance open the door to godliness, that godliness compels you to be kind and loving, and that within that capacity are lights to direct you in your search for this gift from the Father.

Thank you for sharing this journey with me. God accepts the seeking heart wherever it happens to be on His continuum. Change is often the necessary result of enlightenment and sometimes its precursor. May God bless and keep you.

Author Comments

There are many topics I would have enjoyed sharing with you, but I felt that I was led to this one regarding the Holy Spirit and the place He has in our lives and how that place, that niche, has a bearing on our spirituality. Although the relationship of the Father, Son, and Spirit is difficult to understand, there are elements within it that are fairly rudimentary. I know from their repeated statements that they are one, and I am convinced that their purpose is one, having the same goals and compassion for man, who was created for the purpose of having fellowship with the triune God. That purpose is their distinguishing characteristic, but in effect, they seem to have somewhat different roles within their oneness that we recognize as the Trinity. Whether or not this is a fact of their oneness or simply a lack of human understanding does not disturb me. This is because the ambiguities presented do not conflict with God's teaching, and we are told repeatedly that they *are* one, just as Jesus also tells us that He *always* does the will of the Father.

I have not excluded the Father or the Son from this discussion when they are necessary for understanding any issue, but this study was primarily a look at the Holy Spirit. Our interactions with Him included the indwelling preparation of the body to be filled with the Spirit, as well as the ability to change ourselves from the concept of practicing "religion" to learning to be spiritual. This allows others who are outside of Christ to see Him in our lives as something to be desired, rather than scorned.

This type of commitment is a personal matter, one that is done individually. Of course, your walk with the Lord is already understood to be a personal commitment, but when you think about going further than that initial commitment and actually work on your inner person, it becomes even more personal. The will to undergo this inner searching can be compared in the world of nature to the metamorphosis of a butterfly. As a Christian, this process brings to you the transformation that will allow you to shed the old man within and take on a new man, patterned after our Lord and Savior Jesus Christ. This personal relationship is like nothing else in the world and involves not only motivation for the change but knowledge, wherein you must be able to upgrade priorities and decisions, have awareness of your inner person and be able to assess it, and have the ability to transfer your religious life to a spiritual one. This is what living in the Spirit is about.

Perhaps the most difficult of all ideas that must be fully grasped is the realization that God really meant it when He says, "Do not lie to one another since you have put off the old man with his deeds, and have put on the new man who is renewed in knowledge according to the image of Him who created him" (Colossians 3:9–10). Yes, Jesus meant it when He made this statement, so now it is necessary that we utilize His instructions as a priority, in order to learn what we need to know and do, within the bounds of this "new man," who is each of us. We must, at the same time, research to verify both our own understandings and that which comes from the mouths of others, whether it is oral or read.

You don't want someone else making false conclusions for you. It is bad enough that we often do that for ourselves. As a result, I have relied almost entirely on the inspired Word of God as my source. If I do not give a reference, the information is from my own studying and a lifetime of sitting at the feet of many teachers who guard their speech in the manner described.

God does not leave us on our own to accomplish this goal. He gives us tools by which to aid the transition, as well as words of wisdom. Most important, He gives the Holy Spirit as comforter, teacher, and guide. We are not alone. The amazing fact of this whole study is the Holy Spirit and that He waits patiently for our desire to learn what is waiting for consumption.

Let me share a quotation from a small book by Abraham Joshua Heschel, a Jew who lost his family in Nazi Germany. In life, Mr. Heschel walked with God, and in death, he died in God. About living in the Spirit, he said of how we receive the ineffable, "Apathy turns to splendor unawares. The ineffable has shuddered itself into the soul. It has entered our consciousness like a ray of light passing into a lake. Refraction of that penetrating ray brings about a turning in our mind. We are penetrated by His insight. We cannot think any more as if He were there and we here. He is both there and here. He is not a *being* (as we know beings) but a being in and beyond all beings."[31]

Before I say good-bye, I would like you to notice that Mr. Heschel and Mr. Tozer and I all have different convictions regarding an aspect of the Spirit's nature, and that is okay. We are not required to be robots quoting each other's beliefs, because each is someone of whom you think highly. I think highly of both of these men, but if I could read all of their writings, I would not necessarily agree with all they had to say, nor they with each other or with me. This is not a reason to harbor animosity. There are, however, things that must be believed—the incarnation, Jesus' life on earth, His death on the cross, and His glorious resurrection, followed by His ascension back into heaven, where He is seated at the right hand of God. There is so much to gain when faith grows stronger. One of Mr. Heschel's quotations says simply, "God is of no importance unless He is of supreme importance,"[32] and I couldn't agree more. He is saying that the Holy Father *must* be first in our lives. Knowing this, let us seek Him where He is, so that we may know Him better and therefore fulfill His desire for us.

---

[31] Heschel, *I Asked for Wonder,* 198

[32] Heschel, *I Asked for Wonder,* 198

Printed in the United States
By Bookmasters